CLARENCE DARROW

THE CHELSEA HOUSE LIBRARY OF BIOGRAPHY

CLARENCE DARROW

JOHN E. DRIEMEN

Chelsea House Publishers

New York • Philadelphia

CHELSEA HOUSE PUBLISHERS

Editor-in-Chief Remmel Nunn
Managing Editor Karyn Gullen Browne
Copy Chief Mark Rifkin
Picture Editor Adrian Allen
Art Director Maria Epes
Assistant Art Director Howard Brotman
Manufacturing Director Gerald Levine
Systems Manager Lindsey Ottman
Production Manager Joseph Romano
Production Coordinator Marie Claire Cebrián

The Chelsea House Library of Biography
Senior Editor Kathy Kuhtz

Staff for ***CLARENCE DARROW***
Associate Editor Wendy Murray
Senior Copy Editor Laurie Kahn
Editorial Assistants Tamar Levovitz, Isabelle Kaplan
Picture Researcher Diana Gongora
Designer Basia Niemczyc
Cover Illustration Shelley Pritchett

Printed and bound in Mexico.

First Printing

1   3   5   7   9   8   6   4   2

Library of Congress Cataloging-in-Publication Data

Driemen, J. E. (John Evans)
Clarence Darrow/by John E. Driemen.
   p. cm.—(The Chelsea House library of biography)
Includes bibliographical references and index.
A biography of the famous American lawyer, orator, and author that covers such
historic trials as his defense of John Scopes, Eugene V. Debs, and Leopold and
Loeb.
ISBN   0-7910-1624-2
          0-7910-1631-5 (pbk.)
1. Darrow, Clarence, 1857–1938—Juvenile literature. 2. Lawyers—United
States—Biography—Juvenile literature. [1. Darrow, Clarence, 1857–1938.
2. Lawyers.] I. Title. II. Series.
KF373.D35D75 1991   91-2303
340'.092—dc20   CIP
[B]   AC

Contents

Learning from Biographies—*Vito Perrone*   7

1   A Skeptic Grows Up   11

2   The Big City Beckons   25

3   Birth of a Labor Champion   37

4   Exposing a Liar   51

5   Darrow on Trial   65

6   The Thrill Killers   77

7   The Monkey Trial   89

8   Final Arguments   99

Further Reading   107

Chronology   108

Index   110

THE CHELSEA HOUSE LIBRARY OF BIOGRAPHY

Barbara Bush	John Lennon
John C. Calhoun	Jack London
Clarence Darrow	Horace Mann
Charles Darwin	Edward R. Murrow
Anne Frank	William Penn
William Lloyd Garrison	Edgar Allan Poe
Raisa Gorbachev	Norman Schwarzkopf
Martha Graham	Joseph Smith
J. Edgar Hoover	Sam Walton
Saddam Hussein	Frank Lloyd Wright
Jesse James	Boris Yeltsin
Rose Kennedy	Brigham Young

Other titles in the series are forthcoming.

Introduction

Learning from Biographies

Vito Perrone

The oldest narratives that exist are biographical. Much of what we know, for example, about the Pharaohs of ancient Egypt, the builders of Babylon, the philosophers of Greece, the rulers of Rome, the many biblical and religious leaders who provide the base for contemporary spiritual beliefs, has come to us through biographies—the stories of their lives. Although an oral tradition was long the mainstay of historically important biographical accounts, the oral stories making up this tradition became by the 1st century A.D. central elements of a growing written literature.

In the 1st century A.D., biography assumed a more formal quality through the work of such writers as Plutarch, who left us more than 500 biographies of political and intellectual leaders of Rome and Greece. This tradition of focusing on great personages lasted well into the 20th century and is seen as an important means of understanding the history of various times and places. We learn much, for example, from Plutarch's writing about the collapse of the Greek city-states and about the struggles in Rome over the justice and the constitutionality of a world empire. We also gain considerable understanding of the definitions of morality and civic virtue and how various common men and women lived out their daily existence.

Not surprisingly, the earliest American writing, beginning in the 17th century, was heavily biographical. Those Europeans who came to America were dedicated to recording their experience, especially the struggles they faced in building what they determined to be a new culture. John Norton's *Life and Death of John Cotton*, printed in 1630, typifies these early works. Later biographers often tackled more ambitious projects. Cotton Mather's *Magnalia Christi Americana*, published in 1702, accounted for the lives of more than 70 ministers and political leaders. In addition, a biographical literature around the theme of Indian captivity had considerable popularity. Soon after the American Revolution and the organization of the United States of America, Americans were treated to a large outpouring of biographies about such figures as Benjamin Franklin, George Washington, Thomas Jefferson, and Aaron Burr, among others. These particular works served to build a strong sense of national identity.

Among the diverse forms of historical literature, biographies have been over many centuries the most popular. And in recent years interest in biography has grown even greater, as biography has gone beyond prominent government figures, military leaders, giants of business, industry, literature, and the arts. Today we are treated increasingly to biographies of more common people who have inspired others by their particular acts of courage, by their positions on important social and political issues, or by their dedicated lives as teachers, town physicians, mothers, and fathers. Through this broader biographical literature, much of which is featured in the CHELSEA HOUSE LIBRARY OF BIOGRAPHY, our historical understandings can be enriched greatly.

What makes biography so compelling? Most important, biography is a human story. In this regard, it makes of history something personal, a narrative with which we can make an intimate connection. Biographers typically ask us as readers to accompany them on a journey through the life of another person, to see some part of the world through another's eyes. We can, as a result, come to understand what it is like to live the life of a slave, a farmer, a textile worker, an engineer, a poet, a president—in a sense, to walk in another's shoes. Such experience can be personally invaluable. We cannot ask for a better entry into historical studies.

Although our personal lives are likely not as full as those we are reading about, there will be in most biographical accounts many common experiences. As with the principal character of any biography, we are also faced with numerous decisions, large and small. In the midst of living our lives we are not usually able to comprehend easily the significance of our daily decisions or grasp easily their many possible consequences, but we can gain important insights into them by seeing the decisions made by others play themselves out. We can learn from others.

Because biography is a personal story, it is almost always full of surprises. So often, the personal lives of individuals we come across historically are out of view, their public personas masking who they are. It is through biography that we gain access to their private lives, to the acts that define who they are and what they truly care about. We see their struggles within the possibilities and limitations of life, gaining insight into their beliefs, the ways they survived hardships, what motivated them, and what discouraged them. In the process we can come to understand better our own struggles.

As you read this biography, try to place yourself within the subject's world. See the events as that person sees them. Try to understand why the individual made particular decisions and not others. Ask yourself if you would have chosen differently. What are the values or beliefs that guide the subject's actions? How are those values or beliefs similar to yours? How are they different from yours? Above all, remember: You are engaging in an important historical inquiry as you read a biography, but you are also reading a literature that raises important personal questions for you to consider.

Clarence Darrow addresses the jury of the Scopes trial in Dayton, Tennessee. The 1925 trial, which was nicknamed the Monkey Trial, tested the Tennessee state law banning the teaching of Darwin's theory of evolution in public schools.

1

A Skeptic Grows Up

ON A JULY DAY IN 1925, several thousand people jammed the town square in Dayton, Tennessee. The thermometer registered almost 100 degrees, but the crowd did not seem to mind. Waving straw fans and mopping their faces with handkerchiefs, they strained to catch every word coming from the rickety platform in front of the courthouse.

They were riveted by the duel of words between two of the men on the stand. One of them, sitting in a makeshift witness box, was William Jennings Bryan, a famous politician who had run three times—unsuccessfully—for the presidency of the United States. He was stripped down to his shirtsleeves in an attempt to keep cool, but sweat still poured from his bald head and down his red face. The other, a bear of a man more than six feet tall, was also in shirtsleeves, his trousers held up by purple suspenders. He strolled back and forth on the platform, posing questions. He spoke in a drawl and wiped away a lock of hair that kept falling over his left eye. Everything about him suggested a sleepy backwoods farmer. But he was no farmer. He was Clarence Darrow, one of the most famous criminal lawyers in the country, perhaps the world. Darrow had spent a lifetime defending the poor, the laborer, the oppressed, and now he was defending a person's right to teach Charles Darwin's theory of evolution in the public school system. Darrow believed in this right strongly enough to have volunteered to handle the case free, even paying expenses out of his own pocket.

From a distance, one might have mistaken the gathering for a carnival: Boys selling cold lemonade circulated through the spectators. Hot dog and souvenir stands ringed the courtyard. Across the front of the courthouse hung a banner that said: Read Your Bible. But this was neither a carnival nor a religious meeting. It was a court trial, being conducted before a judge and jury—and a vast audience. It was the first case to be broadcast by radio, and thousands of people across the nation tuned in to hear the proceedings. Many hundreds more, including reporters, writers, scientists, and celebrities from Europe as well as the United States, had poured into Dayton to witness it firsthand.

The trial had been moved outdoors because of the heat and because the crush of the people threatened to collapse the floor of the courtroom. Playing on Bryan's belief that the theory of evolution asserts that humans descended from the apes, the case became known as the Monkey Trial. It was one of the most reported, most famous court cases in American history.

The whole affair had come about in response to a Tennessee state law, enacted earlier that year, that made it illegal to teach the theory of evolution in public schools. The theory, which asserts that human beings evolved over thousands of years from a lower order of mammals, was deemed criminal by the Tennessee legislature because it challenged the biblical story of Creation: that God created the earth, man and woman, and all living creatures in exactly six days.

Although Fundamentalists embraced the new statute, many people—scientists and teachers among them—felt it was unconstitutional, a violation of free speech. In fact, a high school biology teacher in Dayton, John T. Scopes, had volunteered to break the law by teaching evolution so that a court trial would ensue. The judge and jury would then, he hoped, overturn the law. But neither Scopes nor the liberal friends who helped carry out the plan had foreseen that the trial would hit the big time, that the legendary Clarence Darrow would volunteer to defend Scopes, or that William Jennings Bryan, the very man who was largely responsible for the antievolution law, would seize the opportunity to be the head lawyer for the prosecution.

Rhea County High School in Dayton, Tennessee, is the school where John T. Scopes taught the theory of evolution in defiance of the state's antievolution law.

What captivated the crowd that sticky July afternoon was not so much the battle between religion and science but the drama of seeing two great orators—both masters of the English language, both capable of using words with the same flourish and precision with which a fencer uses his sword—fighting to the finish. The debate was all the more spectacular because it was almost unheard of for the prosecuting attorney—in this case, Bryan—to be testifying as a witness.

Putting Bryan on the witness stand had been Darrow's idea. He hoped to show that even a Bible scholar and believer such as Bryan did not take the story of Creation as literal history and that it was therefore not fair to penalize others, such as Scopes, who did not treat it as fact. When Darrow had first proposed that Bryan take the stand, John Raulston, the presiding judge, had objected, saying it demeaned Bryan. But Darrow knew Bryan better than the judge did. He had campaigned for Bryan years earlier, and he knew his old friend would not resist the chance to further his cause, which was to protest against what he and others believed to be not only a threat to the Bible but a

The New York Journal *was one of hundreds of newspapers to give the Monkey Trial front-page coverage. Reporters from all over the United States and Europe poured into Dayton to cover the case, turning the small town into a three-ring circus of activity.*

foothold for atheists (unbelievers) and agnostics (those who are neutral about the question of whether God exists).

Darrow's opposing view was no less deeply felt. He saw the antievolution law as a threat to education and advancement. Earlier in the trial he had declared:

> If today you can take a thing like evolution and make it a crime to teach it in the public school . . . at the next session you may ban books and the newspapers. Soon you may set Catholic against Protestant and Protestant against Protestant, and try to foist your own religion upon the minds of men. If you can do one you can do the other. Ignorance and fanaticism is ever busy and needs feeding. Always it is feeding and gloating for more. Today it is the public school teachers, tomorrow, the private. The next day the

preachers and the lecturers, the magazines, the books, the newspapers. After a while, Your Honor, it is the setting of man against man and creed against creed until, with flying banners and beating drums, we are marching backward to the glorious ages of the sixteenth century, when bigots lighted fagots to burn the men who dared to bring any intelligence and enlightenment and culture to the human mind.

Now he grilled the elderly politician in the intense July heat, sometimes harshly, sometimes with affectionate humor, on many details of the Creation story—from whether Bryan believed that a whale really swallowed Jonah to whether he believed that Eve was truly created out of Adam's rib. It was the high point in Darrow's spectacular career.

What forces shaped this man whose brilliance could have made him rich but who instead chose to be a champion of the underdog and of unpopular causes?

Clarence Seward Darrow was born in Kinsman, Ohio, on April 18, 1857, the fifth child of Amirus and Emily Eddy Darrow. On both his father's and mother's sides, he descended from 17th-century pioneers to America. Unlike the many Americans who take great pride in their ancestors' early arrival in the New World, Clarence always downplayed his heritage.

Members of both pioneer families later moved from New England to Ohio. There, in the town of Amboy, Amirus Darrow and Emily Eddy met, fell in love, and married in 1844. In today's world, Emily Darrow would have been considered a feminist, for she supported the woman suffrage movement, participated in political campaigns, and worked on behalf of various causes in education. On the home front she took the lead as well; she was the practical one, guiding the family through hard times. Clarence once said of his father, Amirus, "He was unworldly and unsuccessful, a dreamer."

Amirus Darrow had studied for the ministry at the Methodist Allegheny College in Pennsylvania, thinking he was best suited to be a preacher. But he came to disagree with the Methodist church on the question of slavery—he was very much opposed to it—so he enrolled in a Unitarian seminary, a much more liberal denomination. He was actually ordained, and the Unitarian church was ready to find him a parish, but by then his reading in philosophy and science had made him doubt religion. Though trained for no other vocation, he was not willing to live a lie. With barely a cent to their name, the young couple returned to Ohio, settling down in the town of Farmdale.

In 1850, the Darrows packed up their belongings and moved to Kinsman, a valley town a few miles away, where Amirus's sister lived. They had three children by then and very little money. Hoping to improve the family fortune, Amirus set up shop as a carpenter and furniture maker, crafting sturdy furniture for the town's farmers. And, like most woodworking craftsmen in those days, he also made coffins and served as an undertaker. Clarence sometimes said, somewhat bitterly, that his father profited more from the dead than from the living. Throughout the Civil War, which began when Clarence was four, the bodies of local young men were brought home to Kinsman to be buried. The grim reality of their death left a lasting impression on

William Jennings Bryan (left) waves his palm-leaf fan in an attempt to keep cool while Darrow (standing, center) grills him on the Bible's story of Creation. The debate between the two great orators was the climax of the Scopes trial.

the young child. "I stayed away as far as possible from my father's shop," he wrote. "Never did I want to visit it [where the coffins were stacked] after dark." His horror of death no doubt influenced his lifelong opposition to capital punishment—the execution of convicted murderers and hardened criminals.

The Darrows were viewed as outsiders by the people of Kinsman. In a town where 98 percent of the population were Republicans, the Darrows were Democrats. In a town where almost everyone was a devout churchgoer, the Darrows were atheists. "My father," Clarence wrote, "was the village infidel, but I cannot remember that I ever had any doubt he was right." It was fitting that when the family was able to buy their first home just outside Kinsman, it turned out to be a house no one else wanted: a strange octagonal structure with a wide wooden porch running around seven of its eight sides.

Clarence and his brothers and sisters loved the house, with its big backyard that sloped down to a creek. In addition to the four eldest children—Edward Everett (called Everett), Mary, William, and Elizabeth—Emily and Amirus had three more children after Clarence: Hubert, Herman, and Jennie. (Another son, Herbert, died in infancy.) Though none of the Darrows made a great show of their feelings, the household was a loving place. As was true of many families of that era, strict discipline was the rule. Emily and Amirus made sure their children did their share of daily chores; they also insisted the children attend church and Sunday school every week. Despite their own doubts about organized faith, they wanted their children to have religious instruction so that they could decide for themselves whether they believed in God.

Clarence's parents' attitude about faith must have rubbed off on him, for he grew up disliking churches and religion, whether Presbyterian, Baptist, or Methodist. There was, however, a gathering he enjoyed: the Kinsman

Literary Society meetings. Every week or so, a few like-minded people around Kinsman met socially to discuss books and debate social issues. All the Darrows participated, and even as a young boy, Clarence relished these intellectual activities.

His parents were also active in the Underground Railroad, an organization that helped blacks escape from enslavement in the South to freedom in the North. On several occasions, Clarence rode with his father in a hay wagon, a runaway slave hidden under the load. John Brown, the famous abolitionist who led a disastrous revolt against slavery at Harpers Ferry in Virginia in 1859, was a frequent guest in the Darrow home. Clarence would have been too young to remember Brown's visits, but he never forgot the slaves he and his family helped.

In 1863, at the age of six, Clarence started attending the district school, a one-room schoolhouse. His father valued education as much as he discredited religion and was determined to make sure that every one of his children took his or her schooling seriously. Clarence, however, did not have much patience for his teachers. They taught by rote; they did not attempt to inspire their students with challenging ideas so much as get them to memorize their lessons. Often the classroom exercises emphasized proper behavior rather than, in Clarence's words, "useful knowledge." In later years, the reluctant student would remark that his school days were "a waste of time."

Fortunately, he was naturally curious and grew up in a house overflowing with books. Amirus could not resist buying the great works of literature, philosophy, politics, and science. Books in Greek, Latin, and Hebrew (which most clergymen studied in those days) filled the shelves of the library and spilled onto tables, chairs, and floors in their home. Clarence's father not only bought all these classics, he read them, often late into the night and to the neglect of his regular work. He insisted his children read them, too—especially Clarence, his favorite. So although the young boy was not a good student at school, at home he was quite a scholar, thanks to his father's guidance and vast library.

School was not a total loss for Clarence. He liked the friends he made there, and he loved playing baseball during recess. The formal rules of the sport had been invented not many years before Clarence was born—some say by Abner Doubleday in Cooperstown, New York; others argue it was first played in Hoboken, New Jersey. Regardless of where the game originated, it swept the country during the late 19th century. Every athletically inclined boy lost his heart to the game, and Clarence was no exception. He and his friends played every minute they could: during lunchtime, after school, and best of all, after chores on Saturdays. In Kinsman, the boys played on a "field" laid out in the town square, big enough, to be sure, but surrounded on three sides by shops, a hotel, and a few houses. Nobody minded an occasional broken window, and the players always had spectators to cheer them on.

Clarence, who was tall for his age, played first base. One of the greatest thrills of his boyhood occurred when, in a game against a team from a neighboring town, he came up to bat in the bottom of the ninth inning. His Kinsman team was one run behind; there were two runners on base and two outs. Winning the game depended on him. After two strikes, he swung the bat, hitting the ball with a resounding *whack*. "The ball went flying over the roof of the store," Darrow would repeat, with the same boyish pride, many times in later years, "and rolled down the riverbank on the other side." It was a home run. "I can never forget . . . the mad enthusiasm when home plate was reached and the game was over. Kinsman had won."

In high school, at the "academy on the hill," as the townspeople called it, he discovered that girls were more interesting than Latin and algebra, and *a lot* more interesting than grammar. Once when his teacher scolded him for being sloppy about the subject, he replied, "Grammar doesn't mean that much. When I have something to say, I

The octagonal house where Clarence spent his childhood is located just outside the town of Kinsman, Ohio. The house was rumored to have mysterious powers because it was built by a phrenologist, a person who ascertains people's personalities by "reading" the shape of their skull.

can always say it." His classmates cheered. These were ironic words for someone who would grow up to be an eloquent lawyer, public speaker, and writer.

In his final year at the academy, when he was 14 years old, his mother died suddenly. She was only 48. Her death filled the family with a sadness that lingered for many years. It troubled Clarence that he had not been more appreciative and loving toward her. This regret may have prompted him to become close to his father; he was very sensitive to his father's feelings, to his father's sense of failure for having never achieved his ambitions.

In the fall after his graduation from high school, Clarence went off to Allegheny College, where his father and older brothers and sisters had been students (though his sister Mary was the only one to actually graduate). The only courses he really liked were botany and biology. "For my higher education," he said, "I came back a better ball player. . . ."

A serious economic depression befell the country in 1873 and brought Clarence's college education to a halt. He completed his freshman year, but there was no money to pay for the next year's tuition. He worked for a farmer that summer; though big and brawny, he hated physical labor. Clarence later boasted that he never again did a day's "work" after that. He spent what would have been his sophomore year helping out in his father's shop, mostly painting tables and chairs. To speed things up, he often skipped painting the undersides of the furniture. Years later, people would identify these partially painted pieces as the work of the world famous attorney Clarence Darrow.

Obviously, there was no future for him as a cabinet-maker. He had to support himself, though, so he applied for a job as a schoolteacher in the small town of Vernon, seven miles south of Kinsman. The family's reputation for being irreligious almost cost him the job—many parents and members of the school board objected to the prospect of the son of such liberal parents influencing the minds of their young. He was finally hired, mainly because the school board could not find anyone else willing to work for only $30 a month plus room and board.

Clarence, who was then 17, stayed at the home of a different pupil each weeknight. He liked the arrangement, for each family treated him as a special guest. "I ate pie three times a day," he said. On weekends he returned to Kinsman.

His 50 pupils, all gathered in one room, ranged from first graders to high school students. A few were older than he. As a teacher, he sought to correct what he thought was wrong with the education he had received. He tried to show his students that he was their friend, not a stern authority figure to be feared. Unlike many teachers of that era, he did not believe in physical punishment as a way of disciplining his students; not once did he strike a pupil. Instead, he used his sense of humor as a tool to engage his students and even as a way to reprimand them.

He enjoyed his weekends at home in Kinsman and especially liked attending the Saturday night debates that ran throughout the year. People came to them from miles around, and Clarence, as he had throughout his school years, loved to speak his mind. He was happy to play devil's advocate, arguing the unpopular side of any given issue. When the debates were over, out came the fiddles and guitars, and everyone threw themselves into square dances and Virginia reels. Clarence's favorite partner was a pretty 16-year-old named Jessie Ohl, the daughter of a prosperous farm family in Kinsman.

All those Saturday night debates no doubt confirmed in Clarence the determination to seek a profession that would make use of his good mind and love of the spoken word. He began to read his father's law books, taking one or two with him every Monday morning, and slowly the direction of his life took shape.

The holiday picnics in Kinsman, which usually featured speeches by prominent lawyers, were another town tradition that fueled Clarence's interest in law. The lawyers from out of town arrived at these events in handsome buggies; they were well-dressed men, with shoes shined to a sparkle. Their prosperous appearance, their speech-making skills, and the admiration they received from their audiences made a strong impression on Clarence.

Everett and Mary, both schoolteachers, and Amirus encouraged Clarence's growing ambition and agreed to help pay his way through law school. In 1877, at the age of 20, he enrolled at the University of Michigan in Ann Arbor.

For Clarence, getting into law school was easier than staying in it. His brilliance refused to be boxed in by rules, and he proved to be no better as a student of law than he had been as a student of grammar. His dedication to his studies was also undermined by his poor finances. It bothered him that his family was paying his tuition when they themselves had so little. So after completing one year, he decided to drop out.

This decision did not mean he had abandoned the idea of being a lawyer; in those days, university law schools were fairly new, and one did not need a degree from such an institution to practice law. A person could be admitted to the bar by serving as an apprentice in a law office, by reading books on his own time, and by passing a bar exam, which consisted of answering questions before a panel of attorneys.

With the help of a cousin, Burdett Eddy, a court stenographer, Clarence secured an apprenticeship in nearby Youngstown, Ohio. With its 20,000 inhabitants, Youngstown was the largest city in which Clarence had lived. A few months after settling there, he took his bar exam. A board of friendly examiners accepted him after a single exam. His speaking skills had impressed them tremendously. At the age of 21, Clarence Darrow was admitted to the bar as a full-fledged attorney.

Darrow returned to Kinsman. People there were proud of his accomplishments but did not take the young man too seriously. Very little actual law work came his way, perhaps in part because he did not seek out clients aggressively enough. Instead, he was busy seeking out the company of Jessie Ohl, his longtime favorite dancing partner. Their affection for each other had deepened over the years; he had spent summers at the Ohls' farm in northern Minnesota and had even scraped together the money to travel to the town of Crookston, near the Canadian border, to court her.

Jessie believed in her suitor's future, and her family approved of him. Although Clarence had no money and did not seem capable of supporting a wife, he and Jessie were married on April 15, 1880, just three days before Clarence's 23rd birthday. The ceremony took place in Sharon, Pennsylvania, at the home of Jessie's brother.

Soon thereafter, the young couple realized that to build a law practice they would have to leave Kinsman. Clarence thought of going back to Youngstown, but his fear of "getting lost" in that big city made him decide against it. He also considered a town in Kansas but finally decided to settle in a place near their families and chose Andover, a town a dozen miles from Kinsman. The Darrows rented an apartment above a store, with one room set aside as an office. To furnish the office and acquire a modest law library (a necessity for a lawyer), Clarence borrowed money from the Ohls.

Law business was slow in coming. Clarence and Jessie took in a boarder, another young lawyer, James Roberts, to help pay living expenses. After a few weeks, the two men became law partners. The partnership did not last long. One day, Roberts, who had acquired some poker debts, disappeared, taking all of Clarence's law books with him. They never saw him again. It was not the most promising way to begin a law career, but as Darrow would do many times in the future, he persevered.

Clarence, his first wife, Jessie, and their son, Paul, pose for this early 1890s portrait. Darrow hoped Paul would follow in his footsteps and practice law someday; his son chose a career in business instead.

2

The Big City Beckons

BUILDING A LAW PRACTICE in a small town like Andover, with its 400 inhabitants, was a difficult task. The problem was not competition with other lawyers—there were only a couple of them in the community—it was that nothing much happened that required legal work. Speaking of those days in Andover, Clarence would recall that a horse falling down on Main Street was a major event. Everything in town stopped; crowds gathered and waited around until the animal was lifted to its feet. People would talk about the "crisis" for days afterward.

Most of the business that came to Darrow consisted of drawing up papers for horse trades and settling disputes between farmers about property lines or about the ownership of stray cows. Occasionally, he would plead for a customer who claimed that a merchant had misrepresented a product. He also resolved quarrels between neighbors over some real or imagined wrongful act.

Once in a while, he did get a criminal case. Typically, it was a charge against a farmer accused of diluting milk with water to increase the money paid to him by a creamery; or against someone accused of selling bootleg liquor. None of this work was very exciting, and it did not pay much. In a good month, if he managed to collect everything owed to him, which was not always possible, he might earn between $50 and $60. Even by the economic standards of the time, it was a slim income for a capable professional.

Clarence did not particularly mind being short of cash. He wanted to live comfortably, but he did not then, nor did he ever, measure success in terms of money. He was, however, bothered by the slow progress of his career. He did not let his restlessness get the better of him, though. No matter how minor the matter, he took every client's problem very much to heart and put great effort into every case. "I had a strongly emotional nature," he said. "I had a vivid imagination. Not only could I put myself into the other person's place, but I could not avoid doing so. My sympathies always went out to the weak, the suffering, and the poor. Realizing their sorrows, I tried to relieve them in order that I myself might be relieved."

Limited as a law practice in rural America may have been, it had its rewards, one of which was celebrity. Small towns were starved for entertainment. Baseball games were great diversions, but they happened only occasionally. A court trial, on the other hand, came about often. No matter how trivial the case, it offered excitement, an escape from the humdrum of routine. It was drama, sport, theater, all in one, and it did not cost a dime to watch it unfold. Often the trials took place in town halls, and audiences gathered from miles around. People took sides; they argued back and forth for days. The lawyers were the stars of the show. Taking center stage in this arena of wit and intellect was more important to Clarence than money.

Darrow also enjoyed public speaking, and it was not strictly recreation for him; it was a very good way for a young lawyer to "advertise" himself ethically. Darrow liked to quote the great Civil War president, Abraham

Lincoln, on the subject: "It is the lawyer's avenue to the public. However faithful and able he [the lawyer] might be . . . people are slow to bring him business if he cannot make a speech."

On December 10, 1883, a son was born to Clarence and Jessie. They named him Paul. With the added financial responsibility of raising a child, Clarence knew the time had come to move on to a place that could offer greater opportunities for earning a living. In the spring of 1884, he, Jessie, and Paul moved to nearby Ashtabula, Ohio, a town of homey cottages and tree-lined streets.

Through his work in the Ashtabula courts, Clarence had made a favorable impression on Judge Laban S. Sherman. Although Judge Sherman was a Republican and the young lawyer made no secret about being a Democrat, the judge recommended Darrow for the position of city solicitor. It was an elective office, but Judge Sherman used his influence with Republican friends to promote Darrow for the job. Darrow ran for election on April 6, 1885, just before his 28th birthday, and won—in a city where Republicans outnumbered Democrats by at least four to one.

The city solicitor's salary seemed a fortune to Clarence: a staggering $75 a month. Best of all, it was completely legal—and expected—for the solicitor to accept any private legal work that came his way. Finally, Darrow had secured a job that gave him the freedom to take on cases that would help him gain a clearer picture of his future as a lawyer.

Getting elected to office whetted his appetite for politics, which was an inviting career for lawyers. To young Darrow, a career in politics was, potentially, a path to glory: ". . . to be elected prosecuting attorney, then to Congress, then, governor, senator, and president." Much later in his life, he would have a change of heart. In *The Story of My Life*, his autobiography, he wrote: "The scheming and dickering and trading for political place never [really] appealed to me." But for now, the prospect of a political career excited him. Politics kept him in touch with people, and this camaraderie lifted the depression he sometimes felt over the dullness of small-town life.

Because he never hesitated to argue for what he believed in, party leaders chose Darrow as a candidate for various offices, even when chances of a Democrat winning were very slim. In 1885, Darrow ran for a senate seat in the Ohio legislature. He lost. The next year, he ran for the prosecuting attorney's office. He lost again. But as Kevin Tierney, one of his biographers, explained, "By running, he kept the Party flag flying and his own name before the voters." That he would campaign vigorously in the face of sure defeat only added to his growing reputation for being unafraid to tackle "lost causes."

Darrow had fully expected each of his political defeats, so he was not especially disappointed by them. On the other hand, losing out on the chance to take on a challenging new office made him feel all the more restless. At the very least, he needed recreation of some kind. The days of playing first base in Saturday baseball games were long gone, so he took to playing poker—for small stakes. "With congenial companions, a deck of cards and a box of chips, and [just] a little something to drink, I could forget the rest of the world," he said.

Still, card playing was a poor diversion for a vigorous mind. He spent many hours reading, an activity that exposed him to ideas that profoundly affected him. One book in particular—*Our Penal Machinery and Its Victims*— had an enormous influence on him. The author, John P. Altgeld, was at that time a lawyer in Chicago, Illinois. He had printed and distributed the book to more than 10,000 judges, legislators, wardens, educators, and other prominent officials. In the book, Altgeld expressed his ideas on crime and the prison system and hoped they would bring about reforms in what he saw as a grossly inadequate criminal justice system.

Jail without some form of rehabilitation or training, Altgeld contended, only made criminals worse. He insisted "that instead of punishing crime, society should investigate its causes and then work to change the conditions that encourage crime." These arguments sound familiar today; they were explosively new at that time. They shaped Darrow's philosophy on crime and, in a sense, changed the direction of his career.

Darrow wanted to meet Altgeld to tell him how much he admired his book. He yearned for the literary and intellectual excitement of Chicago. But he had no plans to abandon his quiet, comfortable life in Ohio. In fact, he and Jessie had saved $500 and decided to put it toward a down payment on a house in Ashtabula. They found a place they liked for $3,500; Darrow worked out an agreement with the owner whereby he would pay $500 in cash and the balance in monthly payments.

Then a small glitch brought about an enormous change in Darrow's life: The owner's wife refused to cosign the legal paper because she was sure the Darrows would never be able to keep up the payments. Clarence furiously tore up the deed. "I don't want your so-and-so house," he shouted, "because I'm getting out of this town!"

His announcement probably surprised him more than it did the house's owner. The next day, still in a bad humor, he informed a neighbor he met on the street that he was going to Chicago "to try a court case." Having said this and not wanting to be thought of as a liar, he took a train to Chicago the very next day and went to see his brother Everett, who was teaching there. Everett encouraged him to move to the city permanently. The $500 saved from the failed house deal would be a beginning stake, and Everett promised to help as much as he could. So, early in 1887, Clarence, Jessie, and Paul moved to Chicago. They found a small apartment on the South Side, and Darrow rented desk space in a law office, where he began to build his practice. Years later, when asked what would have happened if he had bought the house, Clarence replied, "I would probably still be in Ashtabula trying to meet overdue [mortgage] payments." Chance, which he believed determined a person's life far more than fate, had made an important decision for him.

A great fire had devastated Chicago 16 years earlier, in 1871. Disastrous as it was, the fire may have been a kind of blessing. It cleared the way for a fresh start, for new ideas, for the construction of skyscrapers that celebrated the commercial spirit. It signaled the beginning of a great surge of civic activity, as if the fire had ignited the determination of the citizens to transform their small town into a giant metropolis.

Situated in the middle of the country, Chicago became a link and gateway between the East and West. The expansion of the railroads made it the center of the national transportation system. Industries—meat packing, steel, and lumber, among others—grew like mushrooms after a rain. All this wild growth required many new city services, such as street, sewer, and public transportation systems, which, in turn, opened the door to a great deal of political corruption.

Only the chimneys and foundations of buildings remained after a great fire devastated Chicago in 1871. Out of these ruins rose not only skyscrapers, booming industries, and cultural and civic activity but also corruption and labor strife.

Darrow was disturbed by the corruption and by the fact that not everyone shared in the prosperity. Partly because of the abundance of labor, working people, most of whom were immigrants, were poorly paid. In the sharp contrast between rich and poor lay the seeds that would ripen into bitter clashes between workers and owners in the decades to come. These struggles would dominate Darrow's law practice for many years.

One such conflict had burst into open warfare just a year before Clarence landed in Chicago. Known as the Haymarket Bombing, it set an unfortunate example of how certain factions of labor would campaign for recognition and of how management would respond to them.

The employees of the McCormick Reaper Works, a manufacturer of farm equipment, had called a strike against the company. Among other demands, they wanted a reduction of the workday from 12 to 8 hours. Management, with the tacit support of the federal government, denied the workers' right to strike, calling it an "un-American" idea. Several clashes ensued between striking picketers and police sent out to protect the factory. On May 4, 1886, about 3,000 men, women, and children came together in Haymarket Square to rally in support of the strikers. The gathering was staged by a group of anarchists who believed that government had no right to interfere with individual freedom of action. These radicals also believed in the use of violence as a means to obtain their goals.

The newspapers of Chicago and the public demanded that the city stop the rallies. Mayor Carter Harrison, Sr., surveyed the gathering, saw that it was peaceful, and refused to interfere. After he left, however, the police chief decided to disperse the crowd. A scuffle broke out, and an object came flying through the air: a bomb that exploded in the middle of the crowd. Immediately, the police began firing their guns. Some strikers also had guns and returned the fire.

On May 4, 1886, someone threw a bomb into a crowd of labor sympathizers and police in Chicago's Haymarket Square. The bomb thrower was never discovered, but nevertheless, eight anarchists were convicted as conspirators in the crime. The event became known as the Haymarket Bombing.

Seven policemen—among others—were killed; 67 in all were wounded, most of them by bullets rather than by the bomb. One top police official admitted that many of his men were hit by bullets fired from the guns of their fellow officers. The city, and, in turn, the country, rose up in anger against labor. Eight known anarchists were arrested and tried. Although none of them had been accused of throwing the bomb or were even connected to the bomb thrower (who was never discovered), they were nevertheless held responsible and convicted. Four men were sentenced to death; the others received harsh prison sentences.

Darrow closely followed the newspaper accounts of the bombing and spoke often about the tragedy with John P. Altgeld, to whom he had introduced himself upon arriving in Chicago. The two men were deeply distressed by the convictions of the eight anarchists. They saw it as a shocking failure of justice. Altgeld, now a judge, encouraged Darrow to team up with the Amnesty Association, a group formed to try to save the anarchists from hanging. Darrow joined, and he and some other members of the association came up with the idea that if Altgeld was elected governor of Illinois, he could pardon the convicted men.

Despite his fortuitous association with Altgeld, who would become a lifelong friend and mentor, Darrow's first year in Chicago was lonely and financially grim. He earned only about $300. Without Everett's help he could not have made it. Jessie did not complain, but for Clarence, with his need for people, the days alone in a strange city were agony. "Sometimes," he wrote, "I would stand on the corner of Madison and State streets—Chicago's busiest corner—watching for a familiar face. [I might as well] have hunted in the middle of the Brazilian forest."

To assuage his loneliness and to help build his practice, Darrow joined two of the many social and literary clubs that flourished in the city. Soon he began to gain recognition for his speaking skills. The real test of his ability came when he was invited to speak on a program with Henry George, the famous social reformer. George had written a book proposing a single tax on the profits from land speculation as a way to solve all the country's financial problems and distribute the wealth more evenly among all citizens. He enjoyed great popularity with labor, farmers, and intellectuals not only for his ideas but for his skills as an orator. He was a hero to Darrow, too.

In October 1888, on the evening of George's oration, an audience of several thousand packed Central Music Hall. After his speech, he received a wild standing ovation. Darrow, slated to speak next, felt a surge of fear rush through him. Would he be able to hold an audience that was already stirring for the exits? "Introduce me quickly," he begged the chairman; almost before the introduction was finished, Clarence sprang to his feet and launched into his speech. Upon hearing his opening words, the audience paused, then sat down to listen.

With a masterpiece of oratory, he held the audience spellbound. He, too, received a standing ovation. Henry

Four of the Haymarket "conspirators" are prepared to be hanged in Chicago on November 11, 1887. One of the men, August Spies, said before he died: "You may strangle this voice but my silence will be more terrible than speech."

By the age of 36, Darrow had secured a lucrative and prestigious position as chief counsel for the Chicago & Northwestern Railway Company. A few years later, he would give up the security of this job in order to defend the interests of the railroad workers.

George hugged him in congratulations. "I have talked from many platforms since," Darrow remarked years later, "but never again have I felt that exquisite thrill of triumph after a speech." The next day, his name appeared on the front pages of all the Chicago newspapers.

His future in the big city now seemed more promising. In fact, DeWitt Cregier, the Democratic candidate for mayor in the 1888 election, had been in the audience and soon hired Clarence as a campaign speaker. When Cregier won the election, he offered Darrow the position of special assessment attorney at a salary of $3,000 a year. Darrow accepted at once, closed his office, and went to work for the city.

At last Darrow had some financial security. He, Jessie, and Paul moved into a nice house. To play it safe, Jessie took in a boarder. She need not have worried. About 3 months after starting his new job, Clarence was promoted to assistant corporation counsel, with a raise in pay to $5,000 a year. His job was to defend the city in all contested cases. Ten months later, he became chief corporation counsel. At 33, he was head of the legal department for the entire city of Chicago.

He was honest, hardworking, and well liked and remained in the position of chief corporation counsel for four years. He handled countless legal matters during his tenure and won a few important cases. In one case, he sued the Chicago & Northwestern Railway Company to prevent them from blocking entryways across their tracks to the site of the Chicago World's Fair—the Columbian Exposition—which was scheduled to open in 1893. Common sense more than legal prowess won this and many other cases for him. He came to believe that it was not so much his skill that brought triumph as it was that "you can't beat City Hall."

The officers of Chicago & Northwestern were so impressed by Darrow's victories over them—and their team of powerful lawyers—that they offered him the position of chief counsel for the company. They wanted his talents badly enough that they were willing to overlook his radical views and his sympathies for the working man. He was not eager to take the job. Among other duties, he would have to defend the railway against employee accident and damage suits. The law in those days offered little protection for employees in hazardous occupations. To take sides against such victims would be to undercut his loyalty to the common man.

A new city election helped him make his decision. The Democratic party had rejected Mayor Cregier as a candidate for reelection; with Cregier out of the political picture, Darrow would probably be out of a job, as the incoming mayor would want to appoint his own staff. In light of this, Judge Altgeld convinced Clarence to accept the Chicago & Northwestern offer. Darrow was also enticed by the company's concession to let him take outside legal work, provided it did not interfere with his responsibilities and loyalty to them.

So, in 1892, Darrow entered the world of big business, something he had never dreamed of doing. Ironically, it was this conservative, corporate position that would propel him toward liberal causes—toward his true calling.

Employees of the Chicago & Northwestern Railway take a moment from their work to pose for this photograph (circa 1925). When Darrow worked for the company, the railroad industry was in its prime; however, by the 1920s, truck, automobile, and air transportation were beginning to erode the industry's business.

John P. Altgeld, governor of Illinois from 1893 to 1897, poses for a portrait. Like Darrow, Altgeld was unafraid to champion unpopular causes. Altgeld's 1893 pardoning of the Haymarket anarchists ruined his political career.

3

Birth of a Labor Champion

WORKING FOR the Chicago & Northwestern Railway Company stirred mixed feelings in Clarence Darrow. He enjoyed the financial comfort and prestige of the position. He thrived on the fast pace of his workdays, which were spent juggling his duties for the railroad—handling city and state disputes over regulations, claims for lost freight, and cases of personal injury—with his private legal work. He appreciated that he was given the freedom to do political campaigning. But what Clarence did not like, as one writer noted, "was being a railroad lawyer by day and a radical by night."

The radical in Darrow cringed "at taking the side of the . . . company against an employee who had been injured in their service, or against a passenger." Every year, hundreds of people were killed at railroad crossings in the city, and many more were injured; it was Darrow's duty to fight against all claims for damages, even when his sympathies—and the facts—favored the victims. As much as he could, he delegated such cases to other lawyers on his staff.

Fortunately, through his friendships with Chicago & Northwestern's president, Marvin Hughitt, and the company's claim agent, Ralph C. Richards, Clarence was able to get financial awards for many claimants or their families who might not otherwise have received anything. Doing so did not completely ease Darrow's conscience, but it helped.

During this period, Darrow continued his public speaking at literary and discussion clubs. He relished being in the limelight; it seemed his spirit needed the excitement of such evenings almost as much as his body needed food. In addition, he successfully managed Altgeld's campaign for the governorship of Illinois, to which Altgeld was elected in 1892. All these activities kept him away from home a great deal, and Jessie was not happy about that. She consoled herself with pride in his success and with young Paul.

In 1893, Darrow and the Amnesty Association encouraged Governor Altgeld to pardon the Haymarket Bombing anarchists despite the strong public opinion against it. At the risk of "committing political suicide," as Altgeld put it, the governor freed the three remaining anarchists, who had spent seven long years in a penitentiary. (One of the men had committed suicide in prison.)

As Altgeld had predicted, the people of Chicago were furious with him for granting the pardon. The public's anger spilled over onto Darrow, but it was Altgeld's political career that would suffer the more serious repercussions. Despite the backlash, both men remained unified in their belief that freeing the men had been the moral thing to do.

All things considered, Darrow was fairly happy with his life and might have remained a corporation lawyer all his days if his outside work had not involved him in what, for him, were two landmark cases. The first was a trial for murder.

On October 28, 1893, a 24-year-old man named Eugene Prendergast assassinated Carter Harrison, Sr., the newly reelected mayor of Chicago. Prendergast, entering Harrison's house by pretending to be a city official, had fired 3 bullets into the 72-year-old man. He had then walked to a nearby police station, handed over his gun, and announced that he had shot the mayor. Astonished and not sure whether to believe the story, the police asked him, "Why?" Prendergast explained that he had devised a way to build an elevated streetcar system and had sent the plan to the mayor, expecting to be appointed to the job of overseeing the project.

An elevated streetcar system was, in fact, already in the works, but Prendergast's delusion caused him to believe the mayor had stolen his plans and appointed another man, Adolph Kraus, to the position. As later evidence revealed, Prendergast had sent a note to Kraus warning him to "resign or be killed." Instead, he decided to kill the mayor. Prendergast was calm as he explained his actions, but when the police asked him at what point he had made his decision to murder Harrison, he became hysterical. "Are you trying to make a criminal out of me?" he shouted.

Throughout the trial, which Darrow attended as a spectator, the shabby, unemployed drifter insisted he had done

A bird's-eye view of the 1893 Columbian Exposition in Chicago. The employment and profits that the fair generated kept the city from feeling the effects of the nation's economic depression until the following year.

no wrong. "I was justified," he said. "The mayor broke his word; he betrayed my confidence." Almost everyone agreed that this man was, at the very least, mentally disturbed.

Prendergast's attorney, Captain Black, knew his client's only defense was to plead insanity. Such a plea would protect Prendergast under the Illinois law that stipulates: "No one can be found guilty of any crime when committed in a state of insanity." (The problem, which challenges the legal system to this day, is how to define the term *insanity*.) Prendergast violently objected when this plea was used in court, thereby, according to Darrow, "really proving he was mad."

Despite Captain Black's efforts—and perhaps because of the public outcry against the murder of a popular city mayor—Prendergast was convicted and sentenced to be hanged.

Darrow was outraged by the verdict. Although he in no way excused the violence Prendergast had committed, he believed that hanging the assassin was an act of sheer revenge by the state rather than judicious punishment—especially because the killer was obviously insane. Darrow felt so strongly about the matter that he petitioned for a new trial, along with two other Chicago lawyers, J. S. Harlan, who was the son of a Supreme Court justice, and S. S. Gregory. The court agreed to hear the case. On January 20, 1894, for the first time in his career, Darrow led the defense in a trial for murder.

Because there was no question of Prendergast's guilt, Darrow hoped only to save the man's life, not win his freedom. The tactics that Darrow used during the trial would become his signature strategy in the courtroom for the rest of his career: the use of oratory and emotion rather than strict legal arguments in his fight for victory. It was a potent approach, and prosecutors would caution juries not to be taken in by it.

Darrow would, in turn, do what he could to undermine such warnings. In this trial, for example, he retorted: "It has been said that I would work upon your sympathies . . . to [ask you] to go beyond your duty, to violate the law [in order] to cheat justice of a victim. I shall not do it." His words had the power of a drumbeat. "Between this boy and the gallows stands this jury, and it must be by your consent that his life shall be blood." In conclusion, his voice almost a whisper, he said, "Your verdict will go toward making history. It will count [either] for civilization or barbarism."

As impassioned as Darrow's pleas were, they were in vain: The jury upheld the death penalty. Darrow appealed the decision to the Illinois Supreme Court, but it, too, supported a death sentence. His last hope was to convince Governor Altgeld to commute the sentence to life imprisonment, but the governor was out of state. On July 13, 1894, Eugene Prendergast was hanged. For Darrow, it was a day of mourning. Ever opposed to capital punishment, he vowed to himself that no future client would ever be put to death. Darrow received no fees for this case.

Darrow's second major case drew him directly into the battles that were brewing between the owners of companies and their employees. In most major industries, working conditions were very harsh at that time. In mines and factories throughout the nation, men, women, and children toiled long hours for low pay. None of the benefits people take for granted today, such as unemployment and accident insurance, existed to protect these workers. By the 1890s, the movement to organize unions that would lobby for workers' rights was well under way. But management was fighting back with all its might; unions, management said, were un-American and would not be tolerated.

The struggle between the two sides raged all over the country. It was especially fierce in Chicago, primarily because the city was the center of the railroad industry, not

This photograph of George Pullman was taken in 1867, three years after he patented his most famous invention, the Pullman car. The industrialist also developed the concept of the combined sleeping and restaurant car, the dining car, the chair car, and the vestibule car.

only one of the country's biggest industries but its most politically powerful. When a severe economic depression hit Chicago in 1894, the sparks that were flying between management and labor burst into flame.

In Chicago and many other cities and towns, banks failed, factories closed, and thousands of workers lost their jobs. Even those who hung on to their jobs could hardly feed their families on their shrunken earnings. The hard times made the workers desperate and ready to fight for their survival.

Chicago & Northwestern was certainly embroiled in the conflict, but it was through a strike at the Pullman Company, in the spring of 1894, that Darrow became involved with labor's concerns. The company was the creation of George Pullman, an industrial genius. At the age of 24, Pullman had invented a railroad car that served as a coach

by day and converted into private sleeping berths for night
travel. These, along with luxurious bedroom compart-
ments with private bathrooms, brought new comfort to
long-distance train travel.

Like most of his fellow magnates, Pullman, a multi-
millionaire, disliked unions. He conceived an idea that, he
thought, would both discourage his employees' interest in
a union and allow him to control them completely. He
would build for them, near his factory just south of
Chicago, a model city. He would provide everything
needed to keep everyone happy: neat little houses with
lawns; paved, tree-lined streets; parks filled with flowers;
recreational facilities; a church, library, and theater, as
well as schools. No one living in this "worker's paradise"
would have any desire to join a union.

If life in Pullman City was so idyllic, then why did
Pullman employees organize a massive strike? When the
discord reached a violent peak, Darrow decided to find out
the answer for himself. He took a train to Pullman City,
which was located on 500 acres of prairie land. Although
the main street was adorned with flowers and trees, the
houses, he saw, were cheaply built. The rooms were small
and dark; each house had only one faucet and one toilet for
several families. Darrow walked farther into the village,
off the main street, and discovered run-down tenements
surrounded by dirt and, behind them, flimsy wooden shan-
ties. Pullman City was more a slum than a utopia.

Darrow spoke with some of the workers to find out more
about their living conditions. He learned that to work for
Pullman, a man and his family had no choice but to live in
this city built for 12,000 people. Not only could he not join
a union, he could vote only for the Republican party—or
lose his job. Liquor and beer were forbidden in the city.

Actually, the "model" city was a business operation,
designed to put more money in Pullman's pockets. Rents
were much higher than the workmen would have paid for
far better housing in Chicago. Tenants had to pay for their

own repairs as well as for gas and water. The library had fees that were so high that few residents could use it. The one Presbyterian church went broke because it could not afford to pay its rent. Darrow was appalled.

When the economy had taken a downturn earlier that year, a bad situation in Pullman City grew worse. To maintain his profits, Pullman cut wages gradually from $3.20 a day for his top workmen to $1.20. At the same time, he increased the work load. He refused to lower rents, even though they were by then double what one would pay in Chicago. After deductions, some workers found as little as eight cents in their pay envelopes. On this paltry wage they then had to feed a family of five or six for two weeks. Pullman's profits actually increased during the depression.

The workers organized. They asked to meet with their bosses to see what could be done to improve conditions. By agreement with the supervisors, a group of 43 employees came to the head office. Pullman broke up the meeting before it began, firing the whole group and giving them 24 hours to get out of his city.

The Pullman employees had gone on strike on May 11. They had walked off their jobs peacefully and had sent representatives to Pullman, asking him to negotiate with them. Pullman refused. Chicago mayor Hopkins investigated conditions in Pullman City and declared his sympathies with the strikers; more than 50 U.S. mayors sent telegrams to Pullman, advising him to arbitrate.

Meanwhile, other, related disturbances and changes had been occurring in the railroad world. Until 1893, railroad union members—like other union members—organized themselves separately by crafts, or jobs. Engineers, firemen, conductors, switchmen, and others each had separate "brotherhoods." Management could deal with each separately and took advantage of this weakness. By itself, a brotherhood lacked the strength to hold out for its demands. But in 1893 that changed, through the vision and energy of one man: Eugene V. Debs.

Debs was the son of a poor grocer from Indiana. He had gone to work for the railroad at age 15. He loved the trains. Self-educated when he joined the first Brotherhood of Locomotive Engineers, he soon became its secretary. Debs persuaded the various brotherhoods to unite into one organization: the American Railway Union (ARU). Earlier in the spring of 1894, he had led the new industrial union in a strike against the Great Northern Railroad. Unable to combat the united group, the Chicago company agreed to almost all its demands, which had an electrifying effect on laboring people. Thousands rushed to join the new union or to form similar unions in other industries.

By coincidence, the ARU's first convention was in Chicago, immediately following their big victory. The Pullman strikers, who were not part of the ARU, sent a delegation to the convention asking for support. Debs hesitated; he felt it was too soon to risk another strike. His membership thought otherwise. They voted to support the strikers, agreeing to boycott all railroads and to block any train carrying a Pullman sleeping car.

About 20 companies, hit by the boycott, formed the General Managers' Association to combat the unions.

Both the factories and the residential area of Pullman City, in Illinois, are depicted in this 1881 engraving. Pullman proclaimed the village a "worker's paradise," but in actuality, living conditions there were wretched.

MANUFACTURING TOWN OF PULLMAN · AND CAR WORKS · BELONGING TO PULLMAN'S PALACE CAR COMPANY

Chicago & Northwestern asked Darrow to join a committee to lead the fight. Faithful to his sympathies, he declined. A week into the strike, Edwin Walker, an attorney for the General Managers' Association, obtained an injunction from the U.S. government that forbade the strikers from blocking any trains. The association argued that because many trains pulled mail cars, the government had a right to intervene, for it was a federal crime to interfere with the transport of mail. While trying not to disrupt the mails, the strikers ignored the injunction.

The association hired strikebreakers—some of them known criminals—and U.S. marshals to run the trains. Skirmishes broke out, and several cars were set on fire. At the urging of the railroads, the U.S. attorney general, Richard Olney, who was once a lawyer for the railroads, persuaded President Grover Cleveland to send in army troops to maintain order and run the trains. This caused a

In this artist's rendering of the Pullman strike, a meat train leaves the Chicago stockyards under escort of the U.S. Cavalry on July 10, 1894. Darrow and Altgeld strongly objected to the government's intervention in the strike.

bitter feud between Governor Altgeld and the president. Altgeld believed that troops were not necessary and that only he, as governor, had the constitutional authority to call for them. Darrow actively supported Altgeld, and he and the governor engaged in an angry exchange of letters with President Cleveland.

All the elements for upheaval came together on the Fourth of July. Mobs of people, most of them taking no part in the strike, swarmed into the railroad yards, adding to the confusion between soldiers and strikers. Shooting, burning, rioting, and looting soon raged out of control. Seven men were killed. It was never discovered who started the violence. One police report later stated that the U.S. marshals had been the worst offenders, stealing from freight cars and cutting the hoses of firefighters trying to douse the flames. Darrow himself was an eyewitness to the chaos and destruction.

Just three days later, Eugene Debs and several other union leaders were arrested and jailed. A grand jury indicted them to stand trial for conspiracy to obstruct the transport of mail, and for disobeying a court injunction. With its leaders in jail, the strike collapsed. The ARU fell apart, although it would later regroup. Pullman refused to rehire any strikers. Thousands of men lost their jobs.

To provide a defense for their leaders, union members asked J. S. Harlan, whom Darrow had worked with in the Prendergast trial, to take the case. He refused, saying it was the union itself on trial, not Debs or the others. It would be the Haymarket anarchist trial all over again, and he wanted no part of it. The union people sought the advice of 80-year-old Lyman Trumbull, author of the Thirteenth Amendment to the U.S. Constitution, which abolished slavery. He felt he was too old to handle the case and recommended Darrow and his friend S. S. Gregory.

Darrow had reservations about taking the case. It would mean giving up a fine job and security for a case that would pay nothing and leave him with an uncertain future. But given his admiration for Debs, whom he described as "one of the kindest, most gentle, most generous men I have ever met," and his support for the strikers' cause, Darrow felt he could not refuse. He went to Hughitt and announced his resignation from Chicago & Northwestern. Hughitt tried to change his mind, offering a big pay increase and his sponsorship in promoting Darrow's political career. Having made his decision, Darrow turned down the generous offer. Although Darrow was going over to the "enemy," Hughitt even promised to keep the job open until after the trial. It was his way of showing respect for the lawyer's skill and integrity.

Darrow and Gregory, who had also accepted the case, spent months poring over law texts in order to build a defense strategy. Darrow decided it would be wisest to go on the offensive rather than plead for mercy. He would attempt to turn the tables so that it would be the railroads and Pullman on trial.

Debs's first trial, for criminal conspiracy, began in January 1895, before judge and jury and in a courtroom jam-packed with spectators. The prosecution launched the case with a vicious denouncement of Debs, claiming that he was responsible for the riots, for the death of the seven men who had been killed by the troops, and for the destruction of railroad property and was also guilty of conspiracy to prolong the strike.

Darrow was undaunted. He argued that not a single illegal act could be proved against the union officials. He proclaimed that if railway management had a right to organize, certainly the union had an equal right. And what, he posed, were railroad men such as Richard Olney and Edwin Walker doing meddling in government? Were the railroads trying to control government? Debs and the others had been brought to trial only to destroy the union.

Dramatically, Darrow contrasted Debs's generosity in risking his own freedom to help the union with Pullman's selfishness. While cutting wages and keeping rents high,

Pullman had refused even to talk with his workers. While starved workers literally fainted from hunger at their machines, the Pullman Company accumulated profits of $29 million and continued to pay out big dividends to stockholders. To confirm these facts, Darrow had a subpoena served on the railroad tycoon, ordering him into court to testify. Pullman went into hiding to avoid the order. This only strengthened the case for the defense.

Darrow did not stop there; he declared that he was going to subpoena every member of the General Managers' Association and then prove their guilt in conspiring to depress wages as well as to influence the federal government for their own greedy purposes. Just when Darrow was beginning to sense victory, one of the jurors fell ill. Darrow proposed that a new juror be selected, but the judge refused and postponed the trial. It was never resumed. Jury members told Darrow that they had voted 11 to 1 to acquit, or free, Debs.

A civil trial remained. In this second trial, Debs and the others were being prosecuted for ignoring the injunction not to strike. By law, a judge could try the case without a jury. It was beyond Darrow's power to persuade an anti-union judge to appoint a jury. The judge ruled all the union leaders guilty and sentenced them to six months in jail. Darrow took the case to the U.S. Supreme Court. Americans, he argued, had the right to fight for just causes.

The appeal was denied. Debs went to prison, where he turned to socialism. In the days that followed, Darrow read the Supreme Court decision repeatedly. He knew that it was biased, meant to suppress the working class from rising up against the power of industry. But at least the case had helped bring the cause of labor to center stage. Soon after the trial, the Illinois courts ordered that Pullman City be disbanded.

If not a victory in the courtroom, the Debs trial was a victory in Darrow's heart, for it proved to him that defending the underdog was what he was meant to do.

Eugene V. Debs is photographed during a train trip in 1918. By then, the union leader had turned to socialism and was actively protesting America's involvement in World War I. Darrow said of Debs, "[He is] one of the kindest, most gentle, most generous men I ever met."

At the 1896 Democratic National Convention in Chicago, William Jennings Bryan opposed the Republican party's support of gold as the basis of U.S. currency. He and others believed farmers and small-business owners were being cheated by the gold standard, which was mostly controlled by big-city bankers.

4

Exposing a Liar

BECAUSE OF HIS OBVIOUS LIBERAL SYMPATHIES in the Debs trial, Darrow expected his law practice to suffer. Instead, people flocked to his office in greater numbers than ever: workers hurt in accidents; relatives of accused criminals. He did not turn anyone away, even if his client had no money to pay him. Often he paid court costs out of his own pocket. One biographer estimated that he received no fee for almost half the cases he handled in his lifetime.

With his soft-spoken way of talking, his kind blue eyes, and his gentle manner, he put his clients at ease. As one Chicago lawyer said: "He had a farmer's way about him. . . . He talked to a plumber as though he, too, were a plumber; to a groceryman as though he, too, were a groceryman." Moreover, Darrow was one of the very few white lawyers of his day who would accept a black as a client.

He himself was surprised at the range of his legal work. He was at this time a partner in the firm of Collins, Goodrich, Darrow and Vincent and had planned to concentrate on civil and business law, the focus of the firm. Although he maintained his business clients for income,

Darrow took on more and more labor and criminal cases. He grew to enjoy criminal law. He strove to see beyond the crime, to try to understand its cause.

Politics continued to fascinate Darrow, and as chance would have it, the national election campaign of 1896 gave him the opportunity to return to the political limelight: The convention to nominate a new Democratic presidential candidate was being held in Chicago. Having served two terms, President Cleveland was not going to run again. Altgeld, as head of the Illinois delegation, would have liked to be the Democratic nominee, but because he had been born in Germany, he was not constitutionally eligible. The Democrats nominated William Jennings Bryan, a 36-year-old 2-term congressman from Nebraska. Bryan was an unlikely choice, for he had won the nomination in a peculiar way; he had been head of a "disputed delegation," meaning that another group of Nebraska politicians had arrived in Chicago claiming that *they* were the official delegation. The Committee on Credentials had reviewed the matter and rejected Bryan. Convention rules, however, allowed him to address the convention audience.

Bryan approached the podium and began his speech. Within minutes, he had complete control of the 25,000 people in the auditorium. Describing the scene in his autobiography, Darrow wrote: "Not only did he tell them what *he* believed, but he told them what *they* believed, and what they wanted to believe, and wished to have come true. I have enjoyed many great addresses, some of which I have delivered myself; but I have never listened to one that moved an audience as that one did."

In that same election in 1896, Darrow, urged by Altgeld, ran for Congress. The lawyer's popularity with labor would strengthen the Democratic ticket and, the governor hoped, help get him reelected. Clarence ran in a district that was solidly Democratic. Because it seemed he would be an easy winner, Darrow did not campaign for himself; he devoted all his efforts to Bryan and Altgeld.

The Republicans won in a landslide. William McKinley was elected president; Bryan and Altgeld lost by many votes. Darrow, however, lost by less than 100 votes. If he had campaigned even a single day in his district, he probably would have won easily. But he had no regrets. He commented:

> I really felt relief when I learned of my defeat. I did not want to be in political life. I realized what sacrifices of independence went with office seeking. Perhaps I would have spent the rest of my life in the pursuit of political place and power and would have surrendered my convictions for a political career.

Bryan ran twice more for the presidency: in 1900 and again in 1908. Each time, he asked Darrow to campaign for him; each time, Clarence refused. Bryan's obsession with religion made Clarence uncomfortable. Their brief friendship faded away.

In 1897 the firm of Collins, Goodrich, Darrow and Vincent dissolved, in part because Darrow's labor and criminal-law work were at odds with the firm's business and civil-law persona. Darrow, who was now 40 years old, decided to set up his own firm, of which he would be senior partner. He hired two junior lawyers and soon asked Altgeld to join the firm as a partner. Altgeld was grateful to Darrow for the offer, as the 1893 economic depression had wiped out his savings and defeat in the election had devastated him emotionally. The partnership continued until Altgeld's death in 1902. Clarence's good-heartedness extended to everyone in his law firm. "He never had a harsh word for anyone in his office," said a colleague of Darrow's. "If someone made a mistake he would drawl, 'Hell, that's why they make erasers.'"

The pace of Darrow's life never slackened. Almost every night he attended a debate or lecture. Sometimes he gave speeches on science, philosophy, or literature. He rarely requested a lecture fee. His growing celebrity brought people flocking to him; especially the "new women"—early feminists putting careers ahead of mother-hood and housekeeping. They found him sympathetic to their cause and personally charming.

In turn, Clarence was captivated by their artistic and intellectual natures; he was excited by their work as jour-nalists, painters, novelists, dancers, and musicians. The gap between him and Jessie widened. For all his rumpled, homespun, "aw-shucks" personality, he had grown more sophisticated. The social and intellectual excitement he thrived on did not appeal to Jessie. She had remained a simple, home-loving country person.

In 1897, admitting he might regret it, Clarence asked for a divorce. He assured Jessie that he had no desire to marry again but that it might be best for them to part. Sadly, she agreed. They parted without bitterness. Clarence agreed to give Jessie $150 a month as long as she lived—a sum that would allow her to live comfortably, if modestly. Nor did he neglect Paul. They remained close all their life. Darrow paid for his son's education at Dartmouth College and hired him to work in the law office during summer vaca-tions. Eventually, as a businessman, Paul would manage most of his father's investments.

When Clarence and Jessie met again a year after the divorce, he wept, wondering if he had made a mistake. In time, Jessie married a judge in Ashtabula; Paul continued to be devoted to both parents; and Clarence adjusted hap-pily to a bachelor's life.

But once again chance, so much a part of Darrow's philosophy, had other plans for him. In the spring of 1899, he gave a lecture on one of his favorite poets, Omar Khayyám, to a club in Chicago. He noticed an attractive young woman in the audience sitting with his friends, Mr. and Mrs. John H. Gregg. (John Gregg invented the short-hand system of writing.) After the speech he asked the Greggs to introduce him to the auburn-haired lady; she was

Ruby Hamerstrom, a journalist for the *Chicago Evening Post*. Her sparkling personality captivated him. He asked if he could see her again. She refused. The more she refused, the more interested he became. Finally, she agreed to have dinner with him, but only with Mrs. Gregg along as chaperone. Alone with her after dinner, he declared that while he did not wish to marry again, he did want her friendship. He was 42; Ruby was 26. The difference in their ages would not matter, he said.

She confessed that she was engaged to be married. They could still be friends, he argued. She broke off her engagement, and they became inseparable. Later, she admitted that she had fallen in love with Darrow at their first meeting. Her vivacity, wit, and intellectuality, as well as her skill as a hostess and gourmet cook, made her indispensable to him. After four years of courtship, they were married in a quiet, almost secret ceremony at the Greggs' home in Chicago, on July 16, 1903.

Three happy months of honeymooning in Europe followed. During their travels, Clarence found time to finish his first major book, a novel based on his own growing up, which was published under the title *Farmington*. Ruby continued her own writing for a time, but soon gave that up to devote herself to her famous husband. It was a happy marriage. They got along well, as Clarence joked to a friend, "because we both love Darrow."

Labor-dispute cases now dominated Darrow's career. As leader of a commission appointed by President Theodore Roosevelt, he helped settle a dispute between owners and coal miners in Pennsylvania, managing to avoid a strike. The miners did not win union recognition, but they did win a wage increase and a reduction in their 12-hour workday to 9 hours. It was a historic victory, for it was the first time the U.S. government had taken a direct hand in labor negotiations. Of the many labor cases in which Darrow took part, two would stand out as milestones in his

An 1892 photo of a mining village in Wallace, Idaho, depicts a federal troop encampment (foreground). In the late 19th century, when miners organized strikes to fight for higher wages and better working conditions, federal troops were often brought in to quell the protests.

life: One involved murder; the other, violence. Both would take him to the West, to Idaho and to California.

The first of the two cases came about in 1905. On December 30th of that year, former Idaho governor Frank Stuenenberg was murdered by a bomb that had been planted on the gate of his house in Caldwell, a town west of Boise. The citizens of Idaho were outraged; though it had been a full five years since he had retired from the Idaho governorship, virtually everyone believed the murder was an act of political revenge—and most people accused the miners' union of the murder.

The seeds for the tragic event had been planted more than a dozen years earlier, in the bitter aftermath of a miners' strike in the town of Coeur d'Alene, Idaho. Such strikes were not uncommon at that time, when the tension between management and labor in the lead, zinc, and copper mines of Idaho and Colorado was dangerously high. Safety measures in the mines were ignored by mine owners, and workers were poorly paid, endured frequent pay cuts, and were not paid in money but in paper notes that could be used only at company stores. When the miners organized and challenged the repeated pay cuts, the managers brought in armed Pinkerton guards to physically beat down the protesters. Then the company fired the workers and put their names on a blacklist, which effectively kept the men from ever working for the company again.

In 1893, the workers had formed the Western Federation of Miners (WFM). The federation's secretary, "Big Bill" Haywood, believed in fighting violence with more violence. Under his leadership, strikes frequently turned into open war, with shooting, dynamiting, and killing. As a result, hatred between owners and workers roiled like a volcano about to erupt. When the miners of Coeur d'Alene went on strike that year, it seemed the state was on the verge of a civil war. Frank Stuenenberg, who was governor at the time, declared martial law and called out federal troops to quell the riots. The army rounded up a thousand strikers, caged them in a barbed-wire enclosure, and kept them there for almost a month before shipping them out to neighboring states. The strikers were told they would never be allowed to work in Idaho again. Governor Stuenenberg, himself a member of a printers' union, had been elected with the strong support of labor. The union people now saw him as a traitor; he became a target for their hatred.

Was the union's hatred of Stuenenberg deep-seated enough to lie dormant for more than a decade and then revive in extreme violence? The police investigating the murder seemed to think so. Two days after the bombing, they arrested a man named Harry Orchard. A "career criminal," Orchard had already been implicated in 26 crimes. When they interrogated him, he could not explain his presence in Caldwell. Police found explosives and enough additional evidence in his hotel room to link him to the murder.

The police brought Orchard back to Boise, where James McParland, a Pinkerton detective, took charge of him. For 30 days, McParland, brandishing a Bible as a symbol of atonement, urged the drifter to confess and ease his conscience. McParland promised him an easier sentence,

Federal troops stand guard in Coeur d'Alene, Idaho, during the miners' strike of 1893. The soldiers rounded up 1,000 strikers, shipped them to neighboring states, and warned them that they would never be able to work in Idaho again.

The aftermath of a dyna-
mite explosion at a mine
in Kellogg, Idaho, in 1899.
The Western Federation
of Miners was not above
using violence—including
shooting and dynamiting—
as a means of intimidating
mine owners.

especially if he revealed the names of other union people who had conspired in the murder.

Orchard finally confessed and, as McParland had hoped, said he had been hired to do the bombing by Charles Moyer, president of the WFM, and by Bill Haywood. He also named three others: George Pettibone, Jack Simpkins, and a homesteader named Steve Adams, who, Orchard said, helped him plan the actual bombing. Immediately after the confession, McParland had Orchard transferred to a private cottage on the prison grounds where he was treated more as a guest than a prisoner.

Moyer, Haywood, and Pettibone lived in Denver and were there when the bombing occurred. Because they were not fugitives from justice, the state had no way of bringing them legally to Idaho. Nevertheless, Pinkerton detectives managed to "kidnap" the three men and bring them to Boise, where they were put in jail, on a charge not of murder but of "conspiracy to murder." The Pinkerton men were unable to find Jack Simpkins.

Adams was arrested in Oregon, where he lived as a farmer and hunter. The prosecutors were eager for a confession from him. Orchard's testimony against the union leaders might not be enough; another witness would clinch the case. Actually, they arrested him on the charge of having killed a claim jumper—someone who tried to steal his homesteaded land—a few years earlier. Because claim jumpers were hated, the law had not bothered to go after Adams before. Now, by threatening him with a murder charge, they hoped he would confess to the Stuenenberg killing. McParland moved him into Orchard's cottage. The strategy worked; Adams confessed.

The WFM hired Darrow to convince the court that Adams's confession had been coerced. This would, they hoped, help topple the case against the union leaders. Clarence and Ruby traveled to Idaho in early 1907 to begin work on it. Darrow was shocked when the prosecution refused to allow him to see Adams, which was against constitutional law. Through Adams's uncle, however, the resourceful lawyer got a message through. Adams quickly agreed: If Mr. Darrow would represent him, he would, truthfully, deny his confession on the witness stand. In retaliation for Adams's changing his story—which weakened the prosecution's case—the state brought him to trial on the claim-jumper charge.

The trial lasted three weeks. The evidence against Adams was skimpy and questionable. Darrow called the trial a "fraud." It was not about Adams, but about a "fight between capital and labor." He accused the state of threatening the prisoner with hanging only to get him to serve their purpose in going after "bigger game"—the union leaders. It was highly unusual for a lawyer to make such an accusation publicly. The newspapers had a field day with Darrow's remarks.

The jury could not reach a verdict; Adams's trial fizzled out. The prisoner was returned to jail to await another trial. The state, meanwhile, decided to go ahead and put on trial

the men they were really after—Haywood and the others—
on Orchard's testimony alone.

Haywood was the state's number-one target. He was
brought to trial on May 10, 1907. To shore up the
credibility of Orchard's testimony against Haywood, the
prosecution had turned Orchard into a celebrity. His confession of 26 crimes and the Stuenenberg bombing appeared in newspapers all over the country. A national
magazine, *McClure's*, published his life story, including
his "religious conversion." Darrow objected strongly to the
fanfare; he accused the governor of trying to influence
public opinion against the labor leaders. Privately, though,
he was pleased to read the printed confession; until now,
because of the rampant corruption in Idaho, he had not
been able to learn the details of the prosecution's case, as
the law ordinarily provides. Now he could plan his defense
strategy.

Orchard played his role as the state's star witness very
well. His story, as Darrow described it, was "evidently
carefully thought-out and arranged." Calmly, soberly, Orchard testified how he and others had dynamited a mine in
Colorado, killing 30 men. He told of several other explosions he had caused in the service of unions; of burning
down his own home to collect insurance, of several other
murders, of bigamy, and of killing Stuenenberg, an act he
claimed to have discussed with Haywood, Moyers, and
Pettibone, all of whom had promised to buy him a ranch if
he went through with the deed. Why was he confessing?
Because, asserted Orchard, he had found religion and
wanted to atone for his sins.

Edmund Richardson, who worked with Darrow on the
defense, led the cross-examination. He attacked the witness loudly while Clarence winced in disapproval. Orchard, as Darrow commented later, remained "cool and
dignified." In fact, one newspaper reported that Richardson's cross-examination only made the testimony more
believable.

In his cross-examination, Darrow tried a different strategy. He teased Orchard into bragging about his crimes, into exaggerating them to the point where he appeared an evil man without a conscience, and a liar as well. Clarence had another card up his sleeve. Long before, he had asked himself: Could Orchard have had his own reasons for wanting to kill Stuenenberg? To find a possible answer, he had hired several investigators. They discovered that early in 1899, Orchard and several others had found a rich copper deposit in an abandoned mine in Coeur d'Alene and claimed it. At that time, Orchard, while active in the union, had also been acting as a company spy. When Governor Stuenenberg called out the militia to stop the rioting during the strike, Orchard was caught in the middle. He had to flee the state, and in doing so, he had no choice but to sell his share in the mine for almost nothing. The mine turned into

All eyes are on Harry Orchard (far left) as he testifies as a state witness during the Haywood trial in Boise, Idaho, 1907. Darrow (center), his chin resting on his hand, believed Orchard was lying to save his own life.

a bonanza. If Orchard had not been forced to give up his share, he would have been a very rich man. Could revenge have been his reason for killing the former governor? Clarence produced several witnesses who would swear they had heard Orchard threaten to do just that.

Summing up for the defense, Darrow emphasized his respect for the religion of others but mocked Orchard's "conversion" to Christianity as a way to save his own skin. The purpose of the trial, he maintained, was not just to convict and hang three labor leaders but "to crucify the labor movement of the world." His voice hoarse, he ended by pleading: "It is not for [Haywood] alone that I speak . . . but for the poor, for the weak, for the weary—who, in darkness and despair, have borne the labors of the human race." People in the courtroom wept.

The prosecuting attorney, William Borah, tried to counteract his opponent by arguing, "This is not a fight against organized labor; it is simply a trial for murder." On July 27, 1907, the case went to the jury. Awaiting the verdict, Darrow could not sleep. For hours into the night he walked the streets of Boise, often with Ruby at his side. A hung jury seemed the best they could hope for. Two days later, on a Monday morning, the jury delivered its decision: Not guilty! A celebration among labor supporters broke out in Boise. It was a great victory for Darrow. Although he did not approve of Haywood's philosophy of violence, Darrow had been convinced of the man's innocence.

A second trial for Steve Adams also ended in a hung jury, and the case was eventually dropped. Pettibone, like Haywood, was acquitted and set free. The state, realizing they had been defeated, released Charles Moyer without a trial. The three union men had spent almost two years in jail. Orchard pleaded guilty, and Judge Wood had no choice but to sentence him to hang. However, the pardon board changed the sentence to life imprisonment, and he spent the next 47 years living in a comfortable cottage on the prison grounds.

During these follow-up trials, Clarence developed an ear infection that resisted treatment. Doctors could not decide what it was. Several times he was close to death; newspapers all over the country followed his illness with great intensity. But he managed, sometimes in great pain, to appear in court to defend his clients. At different times he had to be rushed for treatment to Denver, San Francisco, and Los Angeles, where, near death, he was finally operated on for mastoiditis. After a long convalescence, he regained his strength.

The Idaho trials had cost him more than two years of his life—and almost life itself. The WFM paid him $35,000 for his services; almost all of it was used up by his medical expenses. The financial crash of 1907 wiped out the rest of his savings. Back in Chicago, he had to start all over again.

Darrow (second from right) and his defense counsel plan their court-room strategy during the Haywood trial in 1907.

In 1912, a depressed Darrow sits on the witness stand during his trial on charges of attempted bribery in the McNamara case in Los Angeles. Later, Darrow would deliver a speech in his own defense that would move everyone in the courtroom to tears.

5

Darrow on Trial

IN 1910, THREE YEARS AFTER HIS TROUBLES IN IDAHO, Darrow headed west again, to Los Angeles, to participate in another business-versus-labor battle. This trial would be an even greater ordeal for him.

At the heart of the clash in California was the issue of the "closed" versus the "open" shop. Whereas unions were organizing and fighting for the closed shop, which would mean employers could hire only union members, industry backed the open shop as a way of keeping unions out. At the time, business had the upper hand. In fact, workers belonging to a union could not get a job. But the union was determined to gain control, and nowhere was this struggle more bitter than in Los Angeles.

Leading the city's fight against the closed shop was Harrison Gray Otis, a Civil War captain who had gone on to become owner and publisher of the *Los Angeles Times* newspaper. Once himself a member of the printers' union, he now hated organized labor, deeming it an enemy of the American ideal of individual enterprise. In 1894 he had set up the Merchants' and Manufacturers' Association to fight the union. So great was his power that practically every business in the city had to belong to the association. When the drive to unionize the city picked up speed, Otis fully expected war to break out. To be prepared, he had a small cannon fitted onto his car. As a tribute to the publisher's warlike attitude, his supporters called him "General Otis," a name he was called from then on.

Otis's prediction of violence proved correct: At one o'clock on the morning of October 10, 1910, two explosions rocked the *Times* building, each carrying the force of a small earthquake. A fire broke out. More than 100 people were at work getting out the morning edition. Twenty-one died; more than 40 were injured, some while trying to escape the fire.

Somehow the *Los Angeles Times* managed to print a paper that day, with the headline UNIONIST BOMBS WRECK TIMES. In a front-page editorial, General Otis called the workers "anarchist scum." Labor leaders returned the fire: Led by Eugene Debs, they accused Otis of arranging the bombings himself to discredit unionism. Initially, neither side had any real evidence, but the charges and counter-charges split the country. Business sympathizers were convinced that labor would not hesitate to use violence for its own purposes; workers refused to believe their own people would kill to win.

Under pressure from General Otis, the mayor of Los Angeles hired the William J. Burns Detective Agency to investigate. Other dynamitings of businesses had occurred around the country, and Burns traced some of the explosives used in the *Times* bombing to the offices of the Structural Iron Workers Union in Indianapolis, Indiana. In April 1911, he arrested the union's secretary, John J. McNamara, in Indiana. Meanwhile, in Detroit, other Burns detectives arrested John's brother James and another union man, Ortie McManigal. In what was almost a replay of the Haywood case in Idaho, the three men were "kidnapped" and brought to Los Angeles to be held for trial.

Because of the similarities to the Haywood affair, labor people were sure of the McNamaras' innocence—and were convinced that only Clarence Darrow could provide the two men with the best possible defense. Samuel Gompers, president of the American Federation of Labor, personally went to Chicago to recruit Darrow.

Darrow told Gompers he could not take the case. He was 54 years old, tired, and still ailing from the ear infection. His partnership—now with Edgar Lee Masters and Francis Wilson—was bringing in a fair income, but his finances were still in poor shape. The trial, he knew, would be long and costly. He felt he had fought enough of labor's battles and that it would be wiser to have a younger and more vigorous man take the helm.

Gompers, however, would not give up on Darrow. He offered him some compelling reasons why he should accept the case: If the great champion of labor refused to defend men whom Gompers believed innocent, it would make them seem guilty. Innocent or not, they might face the death penalty. Also, Gompers promised Darrow that he would be well taken care of financially—every union member would contribute 25 cents toward a $400,000 "war chest." Undying sympathy for the working man, plus the prospect of a good fee and of again being in the national spotlight, won Darrow over. Ruby was devastated by his decision but loyally followed him to Los Angeles for what promised to be a long stay.

Even before Clarence and Ruby reached California, the defense had suffered a major blow: Ortie McManigal confessed that he had, with the McNamaras, planned and executed the *Times* bombing. Darrow went to meet the McNamaras as soon as he arrived in Los Angeles. Despite McManigal's confession, Darrow believed the two brothers were innocent. John, 28, and James, 27, were church-going Catholics, active in the Knights of Columbus, a Catholic Society that supports social and educational concerns. Nothing in their personalities suggested violence.

In preparation for the trial, both the prosecution and the defense assembled teams of many people: a multitude of lawyers as well as investigators to track down evidence and to check on prospective jurors to uncover their prejudices. Both sides spied on each other relentlessly. One Burns detective even managed to worm his way into the Darrow team to relay information to the prosecution. A great deal of money was used to pay "expenses," which included everything from legitimate services to more surreptitious deals, such as when a member of one team would sell secrets to the other side.

Darrow rented almost an entire floor of a building on the corner of Second and Main streets and put together a first-rate legal team. In addition, he brought in John Harrington, a former policeman from Chicago, to head up his staff of investigators and hired Bert Franklin, a former U.S. marshal, to be in charge of investigating all prospective jurors.

To offset McManigal's confession, Darrow planned to raise doubts as to the cause of the explosion; one theory the defense held was that it had been sparked by a gas leak, not a bomb. Also, Darrow hoped to prove that the victims died not as a result of the explosion but because they had been trapped by a jammed fire door—the fault of poor maintenance by General Otis. Unfortunately, his investigators could not find evidence to support these suppositions. The more he and his team dug into the facts, the shakier the defense's case became.

The trial began on October 11, 1911. Darrow had bad feelings about it from the start. One of Darrow's investigators learned that in addition to McManigal's confession, the prosecution had obtained union documents in Indianapolis that provided details of other dynamitings. The documents supported McManigal's confession. Clarence was shattered. To James McNamara he exclaimed, "My God, you've left a trail a mile wide!"

James McNamara (far left) sits beside Darrow during his trial in Los Angeles in 1911. Later in the trial McNamara admitted that he was guilty of bombing the Los Angeles Times *building.*

In private, the brothers finally admitted their guilt to Darrow. James said that although John had known about the scheme, he alone was responsible. He claimed to have used "only a little dynamite, just to injure the building and scare the owners; to force public attention to the injustice against labor."

Clarence found himself in a terrible dilemma. Despite their confessed guilt, he at least wanted to save the Mc-Namaras from hanging. But how? Could he employ his often-used argument that hardship and suffering had forced them into an action against their own principles? Might this justify their desperation and win them an easier sentence? No, he did not have confidence in this line of reasoning.

After a sleepless night, Darrow decided to try to negotiate with Captain John D. Fredericks, the district attorney in charge of the prosecution. In return for a guilty plea, he asked, would the state settle for a lighter sentence? Fredericks agreed. For him, the offer carried several benefits. The deal would probably lose the election for Job Harriman, a socialist running for mayor of Los Angeles. Harriman, using the McNamara case as a kind of battle cry, had the overwhelming support of the workers; their votes promised him the election. If, however, the McNamaras

Darrow is photographed with Ortie McManigal's wife and family in Los Angeles in 1912. Ortie McManigal confessed that he had, with the McNamara brothers, planned and executed the Times *bombing. Darrow always showed great sympathy for the relatives of the accused.*

confessed in court, labor, disillusioned by the scandal, would be unlikely to vote for the socialist.

Also, Fredericks knew that a deal would make Darrow look bad; he could not pass up an opportunity to crush the liberal lawyer. In return for their open confession, Fredericks assured Darrow that the McNamaras would not be executed. James would serve a life sentence; John, 10 years. (Actually, John received 15 years.) Given the secret-swapping atmosphere of the case, it was miraculous that this private negotiation was not leaked to the press or any other interested parties.

On December 1, 1911, the McNamara brothers were brought into court in handcuffs. When Darrow pleaded them guilty, an eerie silence blanketed the room. A moment later, pandemonium broke loose. Word spread to the crowd of labor supporters on the streets outside. A tidal wave of anger—directed at Darrow—surged toward the courthouse doors. A policeman offered to take the lawyer out a back door to protect his safety. He refused. "They cheered me when I came in," he said. "I'll go out the same way." As he emerged from the building, broken in spirit, endless cries of "Traitor!" rang out.

Labor's anger stemmed not so much from the confession of guilt as from the feeling that Darrow had betrayed the cause by not continuing to defend the McNamaras despite their guilt. He became the focus of their disappointment, and perhaps their shame. Even Samuel Gompers turned against him.

More serious problems threatened Darrow. On November 28, the day after Darrow had wrapped up the deal with Fredericks, and two days before the McNamaras pleaded guilty, Bert Franklin (who did not know that the trial had been averted) was arrested in the act of trying to bribe a potential juror named George Lockwood.

It was not a chance arrest. A few days earlier, after being offered $4,000 for a vote of "not guilty" should he be a juror in the McNamara case, Lockwood had gone to

Fredericks with the story. The district attorney instructed Lockwood to arrange a meeting and pretend to accept the bribe. Lockwood obeyed and met Franklin and his associate, Captain White, at 9:00 A.M. on one of the busiest street corners in Los Angeles—a corner less than a block from Darrow's office. The district attorney had planted a dozen detectives to witness the exchange. When White passed Lockwood a down payment of $500, they swooped in for the arrest. Just then, Clarence came running across the street; he had received an anonymous phone call warning of Franklin's arrest. The investigator waved his boss away, but the damage was done—the detectives had seen him. Darrow knew immediately that his appearance looked suspicious.

Franklin quickly confessed to the bribery attempt and assured the authorities that Darrow had had no part in it. But Franklin soon changed his story, accusing Darrow of planning the bribery, furnishing the money, and even attempting to bribe another man, Robert Bain, already selected for the jury. A rumor spread that the district attorney had promised Franklin leniency if he reversed himself and fingered Darrow.

In late January 1912, just as Clarence and Ruby prepared to leave Los Angeles, a jury indicted Clarence Darrow for attempted bribery. The indictment was based on evidence provided by Franklin and John Harrington, who had been living with the Darrows.

Darrow, stunned by the accusation, knew he had to hire a good defense lawyer, although he did not know where he was going to get the money to pay him. He was nearly broke. Samuel Gompers, still unhappy about the trial, refused to help him financially. He and Ruby moved into a cheap apartment to save money. The famous muckraker Lincoln Steffens, who was in town covering the trial, offered to try to get the district attorney to drop all charges. Clarence refused. That would not settle his guilt or innocence. He would stand trial.

Darrow hired Earl Rogers, who had been an investigator for the prosecution in the McNamara case, as his chief defender. Rogers was an odd choice, for the men were very different: Clarence was rumpled, casual, easygoing about legalities; Rogers was a fashionable dresser, fastidious, and strict on legal matters. Ruby was not comfortable with her husband's choice.

The trial began on May 15, 1912. A mountain of damaging evidence quickly stacked up against Darrow. Franklin was a member of his staff and was on his payroll. The investigator had no other source of income. Would he use $4,000 of his own money to bribe a witness? And why? Surely only someone with something to gain would be behind this scheme. Who else but Darrow?

John Harrington testified on behalf of the prosecution, too. Why he turned against his employer was also never explained. But while still living with the Darrows, he had cooperated with the district attorney by planting a dictating machine in the house in order to record several conversations between himself and his unsuspecting host. Nothing in the recordings specifically mentioned bribery, but some of Darrow's words could be interpreted as giving Harrington authority to use his influence, in any way possible, on witnesses and jurors. When this "evidence" was presented in court, Darrow burst out bitterly: "A man sleeping in your house, eating at your table, and betraying you! Is there any crime more heinous than that?"

The prosecution realized they had to answer the question that undoubtedly had occurred to every juror: Would someone with Darrow's winning record and honest reputation stoop to bribery? Yes, asserted Fredericks, Darrow had a reputation for going to any extreme to save a client, especially from possible execution. And in a case of such importance nationally, both sides would go to any lengths, even skirting the edge of the law, to win.

The trial went badly. One journalist covering the proceedings described it as "the most violent trial ever held in southern California." Lawyers and witnesses threw insults, and even objects such as inkwells, at each other. Darrow and Rogers quarreled constantly. Clarence wanted to claim he was framed because he favored labor. Rogers argued that such a defense would be fatal. To win, Rogers insisted, they had to break down the prosecution's evidence. They argued about money. Rogers wanted payment as they went along. Clarence had no money to pay him on such a schedule.

Darrow sank into a deep depression. In court, he slouched in his chair like a badly beaten man. Even some of his old friends seemed to be questioning his innocence. Once, while Rogers was cross-examining a witness, Clarence burst into tears. This alarmed Rogers; he was fearful of what the jury would think. He urged Clarence to show more confidence. "You look like a hound dog caught in a sheep pen," Rogers said. "You want me to be cheerful when my heart is broken?" Darrow answered. "If you don't," Rogers warned, "then, you lugubrious wretch, you are going to jail!"

Despite these tensions, the defense managed to score some important points in the courtroom. Why, Rogers demanded, would Darrow want to proceed to bribe a potential juror *after* he had made a deal that had put an end to the trial? The defense was also able to prove that an anonymous phone call had been made to Darrow moments before the bribery. Skillfully, Rogers made a mockery of the prosecution's evidence. In his summary, he asked, "Would an experienced lawyer like Darrow—even if he wanted to commit bribery—trust a man he barely knew to go out and buy all the jurors he could find? Hardly!" His speech was well received.

Rogers, however, was far from confident they would win. At the start of the case, he had agreed to let Darrow present the final summary to the jury. Now, given his client's dispirited demeanor, he wished he had not made such a deal. Darrow seemed in no shape to successfully sway a jury. The night before the defense was scheduled to deliver its final pleas, Rogers went to Darrow's apartment. He begged and taunted Clarence to shake his depression. The next morning, after a sleepless night, Darrow began his own defense.

"Why am I prosecuted in this court?" he asked. "[Not for bribery] but for one crime . . . which cannot be forgiven. I have stood for the weak and the poor. I have stood for the men who toil. And therefore I have stood against them [the prosecutor and business], and now this is their chance [to get me]."

He continued, "If you twelve men think that I, with thirty-five years of experience, with all kinds of clients and important cases . . . would pick out a place half a block from my office and send a man with money in hand in broad daylight to pass four-thousand dollars . . . on two of the most prominent streets in the city of Los Angeles; if you think that . . . why, find me guilty. I certainly belong in some state institution."

He went on, "Once it was decided there would be no trial and no jury, is it likely that I would take four-thousand dollars of money that was sorely needed, and not only waste that money, but take a chance on the destruction of my life and a term in the penitentiary, by sending Franklin to bribe a juror? Gentlemen, if you can believe it, I do not know what your minds are made of."

For a day and a half he spoke with ever-soaring eloquence. More than a thousand people jammed the courtroom to hear him. Ruby sat in the audience, hanging on his every word. As with many of Darrow's jury speeches, almost everyone—including the judge and jury—wept as he made his final remarks. It was one of the most brilliant speeches of Darrow's career.

The judge quickly gave the jury its instructions. They filed out and were back in less than 30 minutes with their verdict: Not guilty. The people in the courtroom shouted, applauded, and wept with joy. The judge and members of the jury embraced Clarence and Ruby. Hours of tearful celebration passed before the Darrows could make their way out of the courtroom. Telegrams of congratulations poured in from all over the country.

But the ordeal was not over. Fredericks decided to put Clarence on trial for the alleged bribery of Robert Bain. The district attorney was even more vicious this time around. Clarence managed to endure the persecution, but once again, his spirits sank. The trial ended with a hung jury. Fredericks made motions to pursue a third trial but then withdrew the charges. This was not an ending Darrow would have chosen; it left a cloud of doubt hanging over him. But at last the nightmare was over. He could go home to Chicago and once again make a fresh start. With one difference: He would never again take a major labor case.

Clarence and his second wife, Ruby, were greatly relieved when the jury acquitted Darrow of attempted bribery. People from all over the country sent telegrams of congratulations.

This 1912 photograph of Ruby was taken after Darrow's trials in Los Angeles were over. She and Clarence returned to Chicago weary and in debt.

6

The Thrill Killers

HIS REPUTATION ALL BUT RUINED, tired and discouraged and badly in debt, Darrow found little comfort in his return home to Chicago. His practice with Masters and Wilson had dissolved. Other lawyers turned their backs on him. He and Ruby had to sell some of the rare books he had collected, and other belongings, just to get started again.

Although his fellow Chicagoans' lack of faith disappointed him, he did not mind the idea of giving up law. Indeed, he welcomed the prospect of lecturing and writing. He was soon invited to speak on the German philosopher Friedrich Nietzsche for a substantial fee. After the lecture, an audience of 3,000 gave Darrow a standing ovation. It was music to his ears: If the legal profession had scorned him, the public still adored him as a speaker. He signed up to lecture on the Chautauqua circuit, which was at that time a popular lecture series.

Just as he was growing used to his new role, a lawyer named Peter Sissman, who had worked for Darrow some years earlier as a young law graduate, paid a visit to his mentor and insisted that he continue to practice. "If you stay in Chicago," he said, "and don't open your office it [will be] an admission of guilt." Though Sissman had little to offer in terms of clients, they formed a partnership.

An eclectic mix of cases came to the new partners. Many black lawyers referred cases to Darrow. Other lawyers sneered at this, saying Darrow would do anything for money. That was hardly true. He often turned down big fees if asked to compromise his principles. As always, he took on many clients who had no money to pay for his legal services.

Criminal law became the major part of his practice. In time, he was able to charge more substantial fees again as small-time crooks brought bigger names to him, including Republican and Democratic politicians accused of graft. The champion of social justice for the poor might have become a lawyer for the gangsters if World War I had not broken out and, curiously, made it possible for him to regain "respectability."

Although deeply opposed to violence, Darrow said that when German troops marched into Belgium in 1914, "I recovered from my pacifism in the twinkling of an eye." In 1917, the year the United States entered the war, he spoke often and vigorously at bond rallies to raise money for the war effort. Still, his skeptical nature never allowed him to be a "blind patriot." "When governments prepare for war," he declared, "the first unit they mobilize is the liar's brigade."

His radical friends were shocked—not so much by his patriotism as by his prowar activities. Many conservatives, on the other hand, were more pleasantly surprised by his efforts and welcomed him into their ranks. But neither praise nor criticism affected his principles. He did not hesitate to go to court on behalf of pacifists who had been arrested for avoiding the draft; he defended people of German descent accused—usually wrongly—of working for the enemy. He publicly supported socialist Eugene

Debs, who had been sent to jail because he campaigned against America's involvement in the war.

But it was most likely Darrow's now well established reputation as a criminal lawyer that brought him, in the summer of 1924, his most sensational case. On May 21, a 14-year-old boy named Bobby Franks, the son of Jacob Franks, a prominent and wealthy businessman in Chicago, failed to return home from a private school nearby. His father contacted the police, but a search turned up nothing. Late that evening, Jacob Franks received a phone call from someone named "Johnson," who informed him that Bobby had been kidnapped but would be returned home unharmed after the delivery of a ransom. The caller told Franks to await further instructions and warned him not to call the police; if he did, the boy would be killed.

A special delivery letter the next morning spelled out the ransom demands: Franks was to board a train leaving Chicago at 4:00 P.M. the following day. At a designated spot, he was to toss out $10,000 in 20- and 50-dollar denominations. The letter repeated the threat that Bobby would be killed if the police were contacted. Frightened, the father quickly obtained the money and waited. That evening, he received a second call—this time, from the police. The naked body of a young boy had been found in a swamp under a railroad culvert near the Illinois-Indiana border. At the morgue later, the father identified the body as that of his son. Medical examiners determined that the boy had been dead even before "Johnson's" first call.

Brutal crimes of this type were much less common at that time than they are today, and so the entire nation, horrified, turned its attention to the search for the murderer of Bobby Franks. The police questioned dozens of suspects, but none of them could be linked to the crime. A few days into the investigation, however, a crucial clue was found. From that point, it took the police less than 10 days to solve the case; to find, accuse, and arrest two teenagers: Richard ("Dickie") Loeb, 18; and Nathan Leopold, Jr., 19.

The facts of the case were hard to believe. The accused murderers came from wealthy, respected families. Like Bobby Franks, they were the sons of millionaires. The families all lived in the same fashionable neighborhood. Albert Loeb, Dickie's father, was a vice-president of the successful Sears-Roebuck Company. His son was an honor student, the youngest person to graduate from the University of Michigan, and was headed for Harvard Law School in the fall. Nathan had graduated Phi Beta Kappa from the University of Chicago and was enrolled in law school there. Both boys had almost unlimited amounts of money to spend. Nathan even had his own car. They seemed to have been given every advantage in life.

It had been Dickie who masterminded the plot. Well built and athletic, he was the leader in the friendship, though younger than Nathan by a year. He had a passion for detective stories and even as a young boy had turned fantasy into action by shoplifting and stealing cars for the thrill of seeing what he could get away with. He wanted to test himself by "pulling off the perfect crime." Nathan Leopold, who was small, sickly, and shy, worshiped his friend. He would follow Dickie slavishly, do anything to keep his friendship.

The two boys spent a month planning the murder. On May 20, the day before their cold-blooded joy ride, they rented a car under a false name. The next afternoon, they drove to an area around a private prep school and cruised the streets, looking for a victim. They then spotted Bobby Franks, a distant cousin of Dickie's and an occasional tennis partner. Unsuspecting, Bobby got into the car. Dickie killed him with a chisel moments later. They stuffed the body into the trunk and drove around awhile, stopping to get some food before heading to a secluded marsh. The two stripped off the victim's clothes, dumped the body, and drove home. They washed the car down before returning it and burned Bobby's clothes. Although they heard the next day that Bobby's body had been discovered, they decided to go through with the ransom plan, never expecting to be caught.

Their mistakes soon caught up with them. In the marsh, police found a pair of glasses with unusual hinges on the earpieces. Only three such pairs had been sold locally—one to Nathan Leopold, Jr., who lived near Bobby Franks.

The police questioned Nathan but did not initially suspect him, as he could establish the fact that he often went to the marsh for bird-watching and may have dropped his glasses there. But other evidence stacked up. As an alibi, the boys had agreed to say they had been driving around in Nathan's car at the time of the murder. The Leopolds' chauffeur, however, told the police that the car had been in the family garage at the time. Also, he had seen the boys scrubbing blood from the rented car. When questioned separately by the police, the two suspects told conflicting stories: Leopold broke down and confessed that he and Dickie had committed the crime. Loeb stuck to the agreed alibi. Dickie was so confident that he would get

Eighteen-year-old Dickie Loeb (far right) helps investigative reporters search a field near the Illinois-Indiana border for a belt worn by Bobby Franks, whose mutilated body had been found earlier near this site. A few days after this photo was taken, Loeb and his friend Nathan Leopold, Jr., were arrested for the murder of Franks.

away with the crime that in the 10-day interval between the murder and the arrests, he had volunteered to go along with several reporters as a kind of investigating detective, to demonstrate his cleverness by reconstructing how the crime might have been committed.

Two days after the boys' arrest, early in the morning of June 2, three members of the Loeb family rang the Darrows' doorbell. When Ruby answered the door and told them Clarence was still asleep, they made a dash for the bedroom. Desperately, they begged the sleep-groggy lawyer to defend the two boys.

Darrow had read about the arrest of the two teenagers. He knew both families, having shared some charity work with Albert Loeb. He could not believe that Dickie and Nathan were guilty of so horrible a crime, and he assured the anxious trio gathered around his bed that he believed the boys were innocent. "But they've confessed!" Dickie's uncles cried out. "You've got to save them from the gallows." The two uncles, the Bachrach brothers, who were lawyers themselves, told Darrow that they would help him as members of the defense counsel.

Faced with the horrible truth about the boys, Clarence was hardly eager to take the case. But he agreed to talk to the accused in jail. When he visited them, he was disturbed that they showed no regret. Their behavior made him even more reluctant to involve himself. Moreover, to defend them would mean standing up against a firing squad of public anger. Fanned by the newspapers, people everywhere demanded justice, revenge, and the death penalty. Considering the wealth of the families, Darrow knew that if he accepted the case he would be accused of selling out for money. But after wrestling with the dilemma for a few days, Darrow agreed to take on the case. In his autobiography he wrote: "In a terrible crisis, there is only one element more helpless than the poor and that is the rich."

The case looked hopeless. Both boys seemed indifferent to their fate; it was almost as if they wished to die. To complicate matters, the state, riding the wave of public fury, demanded a speedy trial. Darrow felt squeezed for time to build a defense and revive the boys' interest in their own future.

Darrow was convinced he could not get a fair jury, for it seemed every man, woman, and child in Chicago—if not the entire country—had been biased by the sensationalistic accounts of the crime in the press. He decided the only strategy that might save the teenagers' lives would be to surprise the prosecution with an opening plea of guilty. This, he hoped, would accomplish two things: It would avoid a recitation of the details of the murder, which the newspapers would rehash in lurid detail; and it would eliminate the need for a jury. A judge alone would hear the case. Darrow, and the other defense lawyers whom he had persuaded to follow his plan, never had any hope of acquittal. But it might be easier to convince 1 judge rather than 12 jurors to reach a verdict of life imprisonment over death.

For this case Darrow chose the strategy of "mental illness." Pleading such instability for a client was nothing new in the game of law, but this trial, more than any previous one in American law, turned on psychiatric evidence. (The *Chicago Tribune* even tried to get Sigmund Freud, the pioneer of psychiatry, to come from Europe to comment on the case, but he refused.) Eighteen psychiatrists and psychologists examined Loeb and Leopold: 4 of them for the prosecution, who insisted the boys were of sound mind when they committed the crime, and 14 for the defense. Each of the experts found a way to slant his opinion in favor of the side that hired him.

The trial, conducted before Chief Justice John Caverly of Chicago's Cook County, began on July 23, 1924. As Clarence had hoped, the guilty plea caught the district attorney, Robert Emmet Crowe, off guard. But despite the

Dickie Loeb at the wheel of the rented car he and Nathan Leopold used in the kidnapping and murder of Bobby Franks. The prosecuting attorney, Robert Crowe, who argued that Loeb and Leopold should be hanged for the crime, stands beside the car.

absence of a jury, the prosecutor insisted on going into all the gory details of the murder in front of the courtroom audience, and Judge Caverly allowed the evidence to be admitted.

The prosecution, demanding the death penalty right from the start, played up the cruelty of the murder. Loeb and Leopold, they asserted, had committed it just for the sport of it, for pure thrill. They were not insane; they knew exactly what they were doing.

Darrow could not plead insanity per se for his clients; he knew that given the boys' composure in the courtroom, the judge would never be convinced. Instead, he sought to show that despite their scholastic brilliance, their minds were unbalanced. Cross-examining one of the prosecution's experts, Darrow won an admission that the boys could have been mentally ill at the time, though not insane. Admitting this, the doctor unwittingly contradicted his former testimony that the accused were sane.

Darrow sits between the wealthy Chicago born-and-bred "thrill killers" Leopold (left) and Loeb (right) during their trial for the murder of Bobby Franks. Darrow was deeply disturbed by the teenagers' lack of remorse.

The prosecuting attorney attempted to deflate Darrow's argument by insisting there was a motive for the crime—the ransom money—and that this premeditation proved the boys were clearheaded. This assertion played directly into Darrow's hands. When it was his turn to speak, he revealed to the court that at the time of the murder, Loeb had $3,000 in his own bank account. Leopold had a monthly allowance of $125, and his father had recently given him $3,000 for a trip to Europe. Money, argued Darrow, could hardly be a motive. No, the boys were emotionally and mentally abnormal. Darrow contended that the way Loeb had led the newspaper reporters through a reconstruction of the crime even before he was a suspect indicated a deranged mind.

The trial went on for a month. More than 100 witnesses were called. Every day, the crowds coming to see the spectacle grew larger. People worldwide followed the trial. Darrow was the star of the show. As one of his biographers commented: "From then on, no living [defense] lawyer could compare with him."

In his summary statement, Crowe accused the defense of pleading guilty only because they were afraid to do anything else and angrily demanded the death penalty. Darrow began his closing remarks on a quieter note, by apologizing to the judge for putting the total responsibility for a verdict on him rather than on a jury because, as he said, the judge "[would] not be swayed by inflammatory rhetoric as a jury might." He went on, "We believe that [these defendants] should not be released, but [rather] permanently isolated from society—alive, not dead."

To make sure his distaste for the brutality of the crime was understood, he said, "If to hang these two boys would bring [Bobby Franks] back to life, I would say let them hang." Then, to clinch his argument, he added, "As for money, if we fail in this defense, it will not be for lack of it but because of it. Had this been a case of two boys of these defendants' age, unconnected with families of great

To save Loeb and Leopold from the gallows, Darrow stuns the people in the courtroom with an impassioned speech about the emotional makeup of the two teenagers and the barbarity of capital punishment.

wealth, there is not a state's attorney in Illinois who would not have consented to a plea of guilty and punishment in penitentiary for life."

As in many trials before, he condemned capital punishment as a practice not fit for civilized society: "For God's sake, are we crazy? In the face of history, of every line of philosophy, against the teaching of every religionist and seer and prophet the world has ever given us, we are still doing what our barbaric ancestors did when they came out of the caves and the woods."

For three days Darrow pleaded, finishing with a dramatic description of the horrors of a possible hanging: the gallows; the boys with black hoods on their heads; the springing of the trap door; their lifeless bodies swaying in the breeze. Neither Loeb nor Leopold had shown any emotion during the trial; now they wiped away tears. Judge Caverly did the same.

Three days later, Judge Caverly pronounced the sentence. Although he had no obligation to do so, he discussed at length the crime and the folly of defendants hoping to escape a death penalty just by pleading guilty. It seemed he was going to order hanging, but finally, he sentenced each boy to life imprisonment for murder and an additional 99 years for kidnapping.

So ended what the media had hailed as the "crime of the century." In 1936, Richard Loeb was killed by another convict in prison. Nathan Leopold served 34 years and was paroled—as a model prisoner—on March 13, 1958. In 1963, he was discharged from parole and died a few years later.

For Darrow, the trial had a sour aftermath. Crank letters flooded his office, threatening his safety. He was smeared in the press for having "cheated the public and justice" of revenge for this terrible crime. He was accused of selling out for money. To Darrow, that was the worst insult of all. The Loeb family had given him $10,000 as a retainer. To avoid the appearance of a sellout, everyone agreed to let the Lawyer's Bar Association set the fee. The Bar recommended $200,000. The Leopolds refused, saying the Loebs had hired Darrow. The Loebs, unhappy with the verdict, finally agreed to $100,000—a small fee for such a case. The retainer was deducted from this sum; and Darrow had to share the balance with the Bachrach brothers. When all was said and done, he received only $30,000.

It was an ironic ending to a case that tested Darrow's philosophy as much as it tried the two culprits. That it increased his fame hardly made up for the slander he suffered. He considered giving up his law practice at the age of 67. He told his friends that he would prefer not to get involved in any more legal work unless he could really "have some fun" doing it. He would have just such an opportunity the very next year.

This cartoon, one of many Monkey Trial–inspired cartoons, makes light of the Fundamentalist view that the theory of evolution asserts that humans are descendants of apes. At the trial, souvenir sellers hawked buttons reading: *Your Old Man Is a Monkey.*

7

The Monkey Trial

IF THE LEOPOLD-LOEB CASE made Darrow an international celebrity, the Monkey Trial in Dayton, Tennessee, in the summer of 1925, truly brought him everlasting fame. Actually, it was more of a debate than a trial, a chance for Clarence to cross swords with his rival, William Jennings Bryan.

Furthermore, Darrow firmly believed in the right he had been called to defend. Time had mellowed his antagonism toward religion. He had no quarrel with churches—whether Protestant, Catholic, or Jewish—whose members did not feel threatened by science. But he objected to any one sect trying to force its beliefs on others.

And, because the trial was to be broadcast nationwide by radio, Darrow saw it as a perfect opportunity to expose Bryan and his followers' mistaken notion about Darwin's theory. He would argue that Darwin did not theorize that humankind is directly descended from monkeys—as the Fundamentalists contend Darwin did—but that all species evolved from a common source.

Bryan, who had become a millionaire by acquiring real estate in Florida, looked forward to sparring with Darrow as well. He was retired from politics, but his oratorical skills were still sharp. As the leader of the Southern Christian Fundamentalists, a group that promoted the sacredness of the Holy Bible, he had fought against the teaching of Darwin's theory of evolution in public schools, as it conflicted with the biblical story of Creation. Teaching students that human beings "descended from monkeys," Bryan claimed, would destroy the faith.

The Fundamentalists had secured victories in a few states. In 1922, a teacher in Kentucky was fired for claiming that the earth was round. And early in 1925, Tennessee passed a law making it illegal to teach anything that contradicted the story of Creation as described in Genesis, the first chapter of the Old Testament.

A few months later, in May, the makings of the Monkey Trial began. A group of men in the town of Dayton gathered in the drugstore of F. E. Robinson, who was also chairman of the school board. They decided to challenge the Tennessee law. Twenty-four-year-old John T. Scopes, a biology teacher in the Dayton high school, agreed to be arrested and to stand trial for violating the antievolution law. One of the group, George Rappalyea, then telephoned the American Civil Liberties Union (ACLU) in New York to ask if they would join Scopes and his local lawyers in financing the defense. When the ACLU agreed, Rappalyea called the sheriff to have Scopes arrested.

But the men in the group had an additional purpose: They hoped the publicity of a trial would attract new business to the city. When the Dayton group learned that the two greatest orators of the time had taken on the case, they knew the trial would put their sleepy city on the map for good.

The ACLU was not too happy about having Darrow on the case. They were serious about challenging the constitutionality of the Tennessee law. They saw it as a viola-

tion of the First Amendment, which, in part, states: "Congress shall make no law respecting the establishment of religion or prohibiting the free exercise thereof." The ACLU would have preferred a churchgoing, conservative lawyer to serve as chief defender. They feared that Darrow, known to be antireligion, would turn the trial into a "circus."

Young Scopes had the last word. "Dayton," he said, "is already a circus, a town filled with screwballs. It's going to be a gutter fight, and I'd rather have a good gutter fighter [on my side]." He demanded that the ACLU accept both Darrow and Dudley Field Malone, a New York lawyer whom Darrow had recommended. The ACLU agreed.

Darrow (left) and his old friend and rival William Jennings Bryan enjoy a friendly chat in the Dayton, Tennessee, courthouse during the 1925 Scopes trial.

As the town leaders had hoped, the case drew international attention. Visitors poured into the city: newspaper reporters from all over the country and Europe; lawyers, atheists, artists, socialists, and curious tourists. The visitors more than doubled the town's population of 2,000. Adding to the confusion were the hundreds of Tennessee farmers and mountaineers who moved about the town with rifles and muskets slung over their shoulders. They were there to oppose what they felt to be a threat to the sacredness of the Holy Bible.

In addition to the Read Your Bible sign that hung across the courthouse, banners promoting religion stretched across many buildings: Jesus Loves You; Sweetheart, Come to Jesus; Prepare to Meet Thy Maker; God Is Love. Souvenir sellers competed with the vendors selling refreshments by hawking buttons reading: Your Old Man Is a Monkey. A circus trainer displayed two live chimpanzees in an empty store, inviting people to come in and see their "relatives"—for 50 cents. Preachers held street-corner revivals and church services.

When Bryan arrived with his wife and son on July 7, the citizens of Dayton honored him with a parade. The Great Commoner, as he was called, announced: "[This] contest between evolution and Christianity is a duel to the death." Endless crowds cheered every word he spoke. When the Darrows arrived two days later, no parades were staged for them, but they were greeted warmly, and many people took care to see that they were well provided for.

At 9:30 A.M. on Friday, July 10, 1925, with the summer sun pushing the temperature up to 100°, the trial began. More than a thousand people, several hundred of them standing, jammed the courtroom, adding to the unbearable heat. Darrow, Bryan, and even Judge Raulston shed their jackets and ties. Bryan's ever-present palm-leaf fan waved constantly.

To Darrow's surprise and dismay, the proceedings opened with a prayer by a local minister, who even prayed for the "foreign attorneys." Before Clarence could object, Judge Raulston adjourned the trial temporarily to allow the scores of photographers to take a group picture.

There was no doubt which side the local people favored. In his opening statement, Bryan flatly declared that the trial was a matter of "science versus religion." Gesturing to the team of defense lawyers, he declared: "You believe in the age of rocks; I believe in the Rock of Ages [the Bible]." Every word Bryan uttered was met with applause. Judge Raulston did not discourage the enthusiastic outbursts. The state of Tennessee, Bryan maintained, "financed the schools and paid the teachers. It had the right to tell teachers what to say and do. Teaching the theory of evolution undermined the religious faith of children. No teacher should be allowed, much less paid, to do this."

Darrow argued that evolution was an accepted science. Science and religion were not enemies, as Bryan had made them out to be. Many scientists believed in God, and many religious people accepted both the Bible and Darwin. The Bible, Darrow continued, was a book of religion, not science. Reiterating the testimony of a rabbi he had put on the stand, Darrow emphasized that there were different versions of the Bible, different translations that could have different meanings. So even in and of itself, the Bible was not a single, fixed text that imparted an absolute truth. This point was shocking to the audience; they booed and hissed Darrow.

Undiscouraged, he pleaded for tolerance, for freedom of thought, to keep the door open for the discovery of new knowledge that could improve human life. At the end of the day, several people called him "heathen" and "infidel."

On the third day of the trial, when a minister again opened with a prayer, Darrow formally objected. Judge Raulston overruled the objection. The crowd cheered. On the fourth day, the state called Howard Morgan, a 14-year-old student in Scopes's biology class. He testified that Scopes had indeed taught evolution, that all human beings

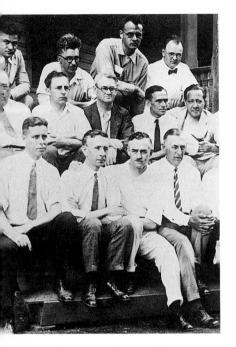

The scientists and lawyers for the defense assemble for a group portrait during the Scopes trial. Later, Judge Raulston ruled that only one of the scientists could testify.

were mammals. The word *mammals* sent a shock wave through the crowd. Parents with children in the room sent them outside, not realizing that their young ones could hear the same words on loudspeakers that had been rigged up in the courtyard. Bryan made an issue of the word. The biology text Scopes had used listed 3,500 different species of mammals, of which humans were one. "I am not the same as 3,499 other creatures!" Bryan roared. The crowd cheered.

A second student, 17-year-old Harry Shelton, took the witness stand and confirmed Morgan's testimony. Cross-examining him, Clarence asked the boy if he belonged to a church. He did. "Do you still belong, even after learning about evolution?" "Yes, sir." "And it didn't harm you?" "No, sir."

Although Darrow's cross-examination showed that learning about evolution had not destroyed the students' faith, nevertheless, the state had proved that Scopes had, in fact, taught evolution and violated the law. Having proved that, the state rested its case.

Now it was the defense team's turn to call its expert witnesses. As part of its strategy, Darrow had invited several prominent scientists to Dayton to explain the theory of evolution; to show that it did not conflict with the religious, or symbolic, meaning of the Bible. Included among the scientists were some noted Bible scholars. Judge Raulston, however, refused to let any of them testify. It was not relevant to the case, he said.

After some wrangling back and forth, Judge Raulston allowed Dr. Maynard M. Metcalf, a famous zoologist, to speak after first sending the jury out of the room. Dr. Metcalf gave a brief lecture on the geology of the earth; that it was millions of years old, not a few thousand, as the Fundamentalists claimed. He emphasized that in accepting the theory of evolution, scientists did not necessarily deny the existence of God. He himself was a believer, a member of a Christian Congregationalist church.

Judge Raulston listened to this testimony but ruled that it had nothing to do with the case of John Scopes. Darrow protested: "Why did the Court favor the State and Bryan so obviously?" "I hope you don't think the Court is trying to be unfair," the judge responded. "Well, Your Honor has the right to hope," Darrow said sarcastically. Offended, the judge replied: "I have the right to do something else, perhaps." At that point, late on Friday afternoon, he adjourned the session.

Over the weekend, the town buzzed with the rumor that Judge Raulston might fine Darrow as much as $5,000— and even put him in jail—for contempt. On Monday morning, he did cite Darrow not only for contempt but also for "insulting the people of Tennessee." In his humble way, looking himself like a Tennessee farmer, Clarence apologized to the judge, blaming his behavior on the heat. In the spirit of Christian charity, the judge accepted the apology and forgave him. The crowd roared its approval.

So boisterous was the crowd that the courtroom floor showed signs of collapse. Judge Raulston agreed to move the trial outdoors, where a platform had already been set up. Thousands of people filled the area: on benches, on car roofs, and in trees.

Once outside, Darrow demanded that the Read Your Bible banner be removed, claiming it prejudiced his case. After much arguing, the judge ordered it taken down. Then Darrow asked Judge Raulston, if he refused to allow science experts to testify, would he instead allow the defense to call a Bible expert? Puzzled, the judge agreed. It was then that Clarence called William Jennings Bryan, his opponent, to the stand.

The Great Commoner, proud of being a Bible expert, was more than eager to accept, to show up his "atheistic" friend. Carrying his fan and a handkerchief to wipe the sweat from his face, he walked to the stand. Beside him, with a Bible on his lap, Darrow sprawled in a chair and casually, almost affectionately, began to quiz his rival.

Did Bryan, Darrow asked, believe that God made a fish big enough to swallow Jonah and then spit him out after three days? Yes, if the Bible says so, replied Bryan. "God can and does create miracles." Did Joshua actually make the sun stand still? Hesitating, Bryan answered that, no, since the earth circles around the sun, it was probably the earth that stood still on Joshua's command. If that were true, Darrow pointed out, did not he—Bryan—realize that if the earth stopped turning, it would burn up instantly in a fiery explosion? "No," said Bryan, "I never thought of that. I have more important things to think about." "What do you think about?" Darrow asked. "I do not think about things I don't think about," Bryan replied. Darrow pressed on. "Do you think about things you *do* think about?" "Sometimes!" Bryan spat out the word. Laughter exploded from the crowd, which had begun to cheer for Darrow.

For more than two hours in the stifling heat, Darrow questioned his Bible expert. Did Bryan believe that Eve was actually made from Adam's rib? Of course. Then where did Cain get *his* wife? No answer. Was the snake punished for tempting Eve by being condemned to crawl on its belly? If so, how did he travel before his punishment? Again no answer. The Fundamentalists in the audience made angry comments, but their murmurs and grumblings were no match for the increasingly raucous laughter that bubbled forth from the crowd.

Perhaps the pinnacle of the trial was reached when the two debated the age of earth. According to Creation, Bryan maintained, the earth was about 6,000 years old. But, Darrow countered, both Egyptian and Chinese civilizations were proven to be much older—never mind the age of rocks. So, did Bryan believe that God really created the earth in six 24-hour days, as those days are now known? Tormented, worn by the heat, Bryan hedged. "Maybe a 'day' meant a year, maybe a thousand years. That was not important."

Biology teacher John T. Scopes (left) walks outside Dayton's courthouse with defense lawyer Dr. John R. Neal (center) and an unidentified man. When the Scopes trial was moved outdoors, Darrow demanded that the Read Your Bible banner be removed so as not to prejudice the jury.

In saying this, Bryan had made a tragic mistake. For Fundamentalists, exact meaning was important. Feeling betrayed by their leader, they actually booed. In anguish, Bryan cried out: "The only purpose here is to slur the Bible. . . ." "I object," Darrow broke in. "I am examining you on your fool ideas that no Christian on earth would believe." To silence the uproar that ensued, Judge Raulston adjourned the session. The crowds swarmed around Darrow. Bryan, abandoned, stood pathetically alone. Even Darrow felt pity for him—and a little regret for his cruelty.

The next day, to block Bryan's closing speech, the defense asked the jury to declare John Scopes guilty. Such a move would open the way for them to appeal the constitutionality of the law before the Tennessee Supreme Court. It took the jury just nine minutes to bring in the guilty verdict. Judge Raulston fined Scopes $100, and the school board immediately rehired him.

The Monkey Trial was over. A celebration and a dance were held to honor Darrow. At age 68 he danced, as one biographer noted, with every high school girl in Dayton. Five days later, on a scorching summer day, Bryan finally delivered the closing speech he had prepared at a church. Then he ate a huge dinner—he was famous for his appetite—lay down for a nap, and died in his sleep. Some people said he died of a broken heart. "No such thing," said Darrow, "he died of a broken belly." Nevertheless, in the pages of the newspaper, the old lawyer paid his onetime friend a final tribute. "He [fought] for his causes with ability and courage. I differed with him on many questions, but always respected his sincerity and devotion."

The Leopold-Loeb trial had been called the "Crime of the Century." The Scopes trial was called the "Trial of the Century." A year after the trial, the Tennessee Supreme Court declared the law forbidding the teaching of evolution in public schools unconstitutional. Darrow had won what he thought would be his last case.

Captain John Thompson, foreman of the jury for the Scopes trial, reads the verdict. The biology teacher was found guilty of breaking a Tennessee state law by teaching evolution, but Judge John Raulston fined him only $100 and the school board rehired him.

Darrow watches the legendary ballplayer Babe Ruth autograph a baseball. At age 74, Darrow was still a boy at heart when it came to the game of baseball.

8

Final Arguments

CLARENCE HAD BEEN LOOKING FORWARD to retirement from law practice for a long time. Worn out by the passing years, tired of fighting for unpopular causes, he longed for the freedom to travel and to write novels and books on a variety of subjects. Now, at the peak of his fame, it seemed the time had come. He was financially comfortable; Paul had invested his father's money well. National magazines begged him for articles, and people flocked to hear him lecture.

But the curtain was not ready to fall on Darrow's legal career. Never again would he appear in trials as sensational as the Leopold-Loeb trial or as dramatic as the Monkey Trial, but at least two other significant cases would engage his special skills.

While visiting in New York about a year after the Scopes trial, he received a phone call from the National Association for the Advancement of Colored People (NAACP). They asked Darrow to defend a black doctor, his two brothers, and eight other men arrested and accused of killing a white man in Detroit in September 1925.

For years, Darrow had been a member and a contributor to the NAACP, which had been organized in the early 1900s to work for the rights of blacks. He had championed blacks all his life, from helping them escape to freedom as a young boy, to defending them in court, to giving a series of lectures at Howard University, then an all-black institution. To turn down the case would be to disregard one of his most deeply held beliefs: that blacks and whites are equal; that blacks deserve good defense counsel no less than whites. He could not refuse, especially because the defendants in the case were so clearly victims of white people's prejudice.

Dr. Ossian Sweet, the main defendant in the case, was a medical doctor who had worked his way through school as a hotel bellhop. Having completed his postgraduate studies in gynecology and pediatrics in Europe, he had come back to Detroit with his wife and two-year-old daughter to resume his medical practice. He did not want to live in the black ghetto and was able to afford something better, so he had bought a house in a working-class white neighborhood. Two of his black friends, a lawyer and an undertaker, had been forced out of homes they had bought in similar neighborhoods. But Dr. Sweet, making no secret of his purchase, was determined to stay.

He took no chances. On September 8, when he moved in, he had the help of his brothers Otis, a dentist, and Henry, a college student. With them came eight other men, bringing several handguns, a rifle, and ammunition. A crowd gathered outside that evening, but nothing happened. The next night, a bigger, more threatening crowd surrounded the house. A dozen policemen looked on passively. Suddenly, stones rained down on the house, breaking darkened windows. Shots rang out, whether first from the house or from the street no one could remember. But one white man on the far edge of the crowd, Leon Breiner, was killed, and another was wounded. At that point, the police entered the house, arrested all the men, and took them to jail without even allowing them to call an attorney.

In mid-October, Clarence and Ruby traveled to Detroit for the trial. In reviewing the case, Darrow was impressed that Dr. Sweet and his friends had had the courage to defend themselves. He did not advocate violence, but he knew the accused men had acted in self-defense, against the threat of mob destruction. Convincing the jury of this would be the focus of his defense.

The trial began in late October, before Judge Frank Murphy, who would eventually become a U.S. Supreme Court justice, and who, in Darrow's view, was a very fair-minded man. To dignify his clients, all well-educated, prosperous blacks, Darrow came to court in a new, well-pressed suit, a far cry from his usual rumpled look.

The prosecution called more than 60 witnesses to prove that there was no mob at the scene, only a few people enjoying an evening stroll; that the shots were unprovoked, fired for no reason except as a conspiracy to kill any white person trespassing near the property. Darrow listened quietly, actually working crossword puzzles during much of the testimony. Then, when it was his turn to question the witnesses, he had a white reporter testify that a crowd of at least 500 people had gathered that night. He also got some teenagers who had testified for the state to admit that they had been coached by the police to lie. From other prosecution witnesses he established that the true conspiracy in the case had not been acted out by Dr. Sweet and his friends but by the Works Improvement Association, a group formed by the neighborhood to keep blacks out.

On November 18, Clarence called Dr. Sweet to the stand to tell the story of his life. Dr. Sweet swore that he himself had not handled a gun that evening but agreed that shots had been fired from the house. Later, his brother Henry admitted that he did fire several shots. But the bullets from his gun did not match those that killed Leon Breiner.

Clarence, Ruby, and a friend show off the birthday cake at a testimonial dinner honoring Clarence's 70th birthday. Some 1,200 friends gathered for the event.

Darrow spoke passionately about the evil consequences of prejudice. This trial was perhaps the first in which the reality of racial violence and its tragedy—for all sides—was openly confronted in a court of law. As in most of his major cases, Darrow spoke not only on behalf of his clients but of all people—maybe, if his words were eloquent enough, persuasive enough, future generations would not face the same degree of prejudice.

The jury could not reach a verdict. The defendants were released on bail to await a new trial. The following April, Henry Sweet was tried separately. That the fatal bullets were not fired from his gun severely weakened the prosecution's case, but Darrow knew he nevertheless had to provide a forceful defense. Again, he brought up the issue of racial prejudice. "If eleven white men protecting their home against a mob of blacks had shot and killed a black, they would never have been [brought] to trial," he said. "They would have been given medals instead."

In less than four hours the jury brought in a verdict of not guilty. A year later, all charges against the 11 men were dismissed. Even the district attorney agreed that it was the best conclusion to the case. Judge Murphy had the last word. "Clarence," he said, "never mouths Christianity but always practices it."

Happy years followed the Sweet trial. In 1927, 1,200 people honored Darrow with a testimonial dinner on his 70th birthday. Their praise made him blush. "Far from encouraging disrespect for the law—as he was sometimes accused of doing—no man has done more to promote it," one judge said. Commenting on the lawyer's reputation for being against religion, a famous minister, Reverend John Haynes Holmes of New York City, said, "In Jerusalem, Jesus had no defenders; in Chicago, He would have a defender—Clarence Darrow."

He traveled from city to city to engage in a series of popular debates on religion. In each city the panel would include a minister, a priest, a rabbi, and Darrow—an agnostic. Although the majority of each audience consisted of religious people, Clarence usually got most of the applause, for his wit and eloquence. He and Ruby traveled in Europe, where they enjoyed the company of many famous authors and artists. It was during these travels that he wrote his autobiography. He was happy to be free of courtrooms. In 1928, Darrow officially retired from the practice of law.

In October 1929, while the Darrows were in Europe, the New York stock market crashed, wiping out their savings and their hopes of a carefree retirement. Nevertheless, Darrow was determined to avoid the legal arena. For four years, he earned his livelihood by writing and lecturing. But early in 1932, still struggling financially at the age of 75, the offer of a $25,000 fee to defend four people in Honolulu, Hawaii, on a murder charge was too tempting to resist.

Five native Hawaiians were accused of raping a white woman, Thalia Massie, wife of U.S. Navy lieutenant Thomas Massie, stationed on the island. When the trial ended without a decision, Lieutenant Massie, with the help of two other sailors and his mother-in-law, Mrs. Fortescue, managed to kidnap the native ring leader, Joseph Kahahawaii. Under pressure from the Americans, he allegedly

Darrow stands with his clients Thalia and Thomas Massie and their dog, Kriss, on board the San Francisco–bound liner, the Malolo *in May 1925. The Massie murder was the last case Darrow brought to trial before retiring from the practice of law.*

confessed. At that point, Massie, in great anguish as he later admitted, shot and killed the native.

The case threatened to explode the racial tension already building in the islands. It was to defend Massie and Fortescue that Clarence went to Hawaii. Throughout the trial, Darrow worked to soothe the anger of the whites and natives. He asked the jury to take into consideration the months of mental strain Massie had endured. The jury convicted the defendants and sentenced each of them to 10 years in prison. With his gift of quiet persuasion, though, Darrow convinced the governor to remit their sentences to one hour if they would leave the islands immediately. This move, combined with his pleas for racial understanding, did much to calm the racial tensions both in the United States and in Hawaii.

Now, after more than 50 years of pleading for justice and compassion for the poor, the underprivileged, the victims of their own crimes, Darrow retired from the practice of law—this time, for good.

Retirement, however, did not mean the end of public service. During the Great Depression of the 1930s, Darrow led a commission appointed by President Franklin Delano Roosevelt to work out some of the unfair elements of the National Industrial Recovery Act (NIRA), a law aimed at relieving the depression. Darrow's judgment and leadership were upheld when the Supreme Court declared the law unconstitutional. Positive revisions of the law were made. In addition, Clarence had the satisfaction of seeing many new laws enacted to improve the life of working people: a minimum wage, unemployment insurance, old-age pensions, and others. Unions again welcomed him as their champion.

His hatred of capital punishment never wavered. Nearing his 80th birthday, he argued before the Michigan state legislature, which was considering a bill to restore the death penalty in Michigan. His pleas helped defeat the bill. "Cure poverty," he said, "and you will cure most crime. If

Clarence and Ruby appear in a 1932 photo, after almost three decades of happy marriage. Darrow once joked to a friend that he and Ruby got along well "because we both love Darrow."

every man and woman in the world had a chance to make a decent, fair, honest living, there would be no jails, and no lawyers and no courts." He could love the sinner even as he hated the sin.

His attitude toward crime would be challenged by many today as being too easy on criminals. Still, his opinions, his oratory, and the countless cases and causes he championed have had a lasting effect on the American legal system. Although there were certainly liberal lawyers before his time and since, none have equaled him in the power of his brilliance and influence.

Old age steadily robbed him of his energy. In 1936, he was able to make a sentimental visit to his birthplace in Kinsman and was saddened by how it had changed. When he was able to, he loved to walk in Jackson Park on Chicago's South Side, near where he lived. A favorite spot was a small bridge over a pond. He could see it from the window of his apartment and found joy in looking at it.

As she had all the years of their life together, Ruby fussed over Clarence. When he was younger, her excessive care sometimes annoyed him a little; now it gave him great comfort. On his 80th birthday, a photographer came to take his picture. "Do I really look eighty?" Darrow asked. "Mr. Darrow," the cameraman said, "you always looked eighty." His old friend, the writer Henry L. Mencken, never noted for being softhearted, had kinder words. In effect he said, "Your actual age is what it has always been, about thirty, the prime of human life."

On March 13, 1938, a month short of his 81st birthday, Clarence Darrow died. His body lay in state for two days at a funeral home. In driving rain, thousands of mourners lined up to view his body and honor his memory: blacks and whites; rich and poor; professors and street people; judges and criminals. He and his friend and onetime partner, Judge William H. Holly, had agreed that the survivor would give the eulogy at the other's funeral. "He knows everything about me," Clarence had said, "and he has the sense not to tell it."

In his remarks—not trusting his own eloquence to do justice to his friend—Judge Holly used many of the words that Darrow had spoken at the funeral of Governor John P. Altgeld many years earlier. And he added, "Thousands of lives were made richer and happier because Clarence Darrow lived." As Darrow had requested, his body was cremated, and his son, Paul, and four other friends scattered the ashes from the little bridge in Jackson Park. In 1957, on the 100th anniversary of his birth, in a special ceremony, a memorial plaque was mounted on the bridge, naming it in dedication as the Clarence Darrow Memorial Bridge. A library in the Cook County jail in Chicago also bears his name—one of many honors bestowed upon him.

In a famous quotation, President Abraham Lincoln (who was still alive when the lawyer-to-be was born) once said: "God must have loved the common people because he made so many of them." Of Clarence Darrow it could also be said that although he saw the weakness of human nature clearly and pessimistically, he, too, loved the common people. He dedicated his life to them. His greatness and brilliance were matched only by his humility.

In 1957, on the 100th anniversary of Darrow's birth, friends, family, and admirers gathered at the bridge that Darrow loved, in Chicago's Jackson Park. In a special ceremony, the bridge was renamed the Clarence Darrow Memorial Bridge.

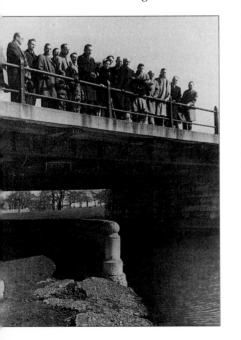

Further Reading

Bridges, Horace J. *God of Fundamentalism and Other Studies*. 1925. Reprint. New York: Books for Libraries Press, 1965.

Darrow, Clarence. *Crime, Its Cause and Treatment*. 1922. Reprint. New York: Patterson Smith, 1972.

————. *Farmington*. 1904. Reprint. New York: Scribners, 1932.

————. *The Story of My Life*. 1932. Reprint. New York: Scribners, 1960.

Gurko, Miriam. *Clarence Darrow*. New York: Crowell, 1965.

Harrison, Charles Yale. *Clarence Darrow*. New York: Cape & Smith, 1931.

Lawrence, Jerome, and Robert E. Lee. *Inherit the Wind*. 1955. Reprint. New York: Bantam Books, 1982.

Ravitz, Abe C. *Clarence Darrow and the American Literary Tradition*. Cleveland: Western Reserve University Press, 1962.

Stone, Irving. *Clarence Darrow for the Defense*. 1941. Reprint. New York: Doubleday, 1989.

Tierney, Kevin. *Darrow, a Biography*. New York: Crowell, 1979.

Weinberg, Arthur. *Attorney for the Damned*. 1957. Reprint. New York: Simon & Schuster, 1983.

Weinberg, Arthur, and Lila Weinberg. *Clarence Darrow: A Sentimental Rebel*. 1980. Reprint. New York: Atheneum, 1987.

Chronology

1857	Born Clarence Seward Darrow in Kinsman, Ohio, on April 18
1872	Graduates from high school in Kinsman; enrolls at Allegheny College in Meadville, Pennsylvania; mother dies
1873	An economic depression sweeps the country; unable to afford the tuition, Clarence leaves Allegheny College after one year
1874–77	Works as a schoolteacher in Vernon, Ohio; becomes interested in law
1877	Enrolls at University of Michigan Law School in Ann Arbor
1878	Apprentices in a law firm in Youngstown, Ohio; is admitted to the bar as an attorney
1880	Marries his childhood sweetheart, Jessie Ohl; they settle in Andover, Ohio
1883	Clarence and Jessie's son, Paul, born on December 10
1884	Family moves to Ashtabula, Ohio
1887	The Darrows move to Chicago; Clarence meets John P. Altgeld; becomes involved with effort to save Haymarket Square anarchists
1888	Wins recognition as public speaker on program with noted social reformer Henry George; becomes chief corporation counsel for the city of Chicago
1892	Leaves city government to become chief counsel for Chicago & Northwestern Railway Company
1894	Handles his first criminal case in Chicago, defending Eugene Prendergast; leaves Chicago & Northwestern to defend Eugene V. Debs
1896	Delegate to Democratic National Convention in Chicago; campaigns for William Jennings Bryan and Altgeld; runs for Congress
1897	Clarence and Jessie are divorced

1903   Darrow marries Ruby Hamerstrom on July 16; they travel in Europe for three months

1907   Darrow defends union leaders accused of murdering former governor in Boise, Idaho

1911   Defends John and James McNamara in the *Los Angeles Times* bombing case

1912   Accused of bribing jurors in *Times* bombing case; stands trial and is acquitted

1917   Supports American war effort in World War I while defending the rights of pacifists

1924   Defends Richard Loeb and Nathan Leopold, Jr., in Chicago

1925   Leads the defense in the Monkey Trial in Dayton, Tennessee

1926   Defends 11 blacks falsely accused of murdering a white in Detroit

1930–31   Stars in a series of debates on religion in various cities with Protestant, Catholic, and Jewish clergymen

1932   Publishes his autobiography, *The Story of My Life*; serves as defense counsel in the Massie case in Honolulu, Hawaii

1934   Serves as chairman of President Franklin D. Roosevelt's commission to determine constitutionality of National Industrial Recovery Act (NIRA)

1938   Dies on March 13, one month short of his 81st birthday

Index

Adams, Steve, 58, 59, 62
Agnostics, 14
Allegheny College, 15, 20
Altgeld, John P., 28–29,
   32–33, 38, 41, 47, 52,
   53, 106
Amboy, Ohio, 15
American Civil Liberties
   Union (ACLU), 90–91
American Railway Union
   (ARU), 45, 47
Amnesty Association, 32, 38
Andover, Ohio, 23, 25
Ashtabula, Ohio, 27, 29, 30, 54
Atheists, 14

Bachrach brothers, 82, 87
Bain, Robert, 71, 75
Bible, 13, 90, 93–97
Black, Captain, 40
Boise, Idaho, 57
Borah, William, 62
Breiner, Leon, 100, 101
Brown, John, 18
Bryan, William Jennings, 11–
   13, 52, 53, 92–97
      as presidential nominee,
      52–53
      and Scopes trial, 11–15,
      89–97

Caldwell, Idaho, 56
Caverly, John, 83–84, 87
Chicago, Illinois, 28, 38, 39,
   43, 44, 52, 54, 55, 63, 67,
   75, 77, 78, 79, 83, 102, 105
Chicago & Northwestern
   Railway Company, 34–35,
   37, 42, 46, 48
Chicago Evening Post, 55
Chicago Tribune, 83
Civil War, 16
Clarence Darrow Memorial
   Bridge, 106
Cleveland, Grover, 46, 47, 52

Collins, Goodrich, Darrow &
   Vincent, 51, 53
Coeur d'Alene, Idaho, 56
Columbian Exposition, 34
Creation story, 13, 15, 90, 96
Cregier, DeWitt, 34, 35
Crowe, Robert Emmet, 83, 85

Darrow, Amirus (father), 15–
   18, 20, 22
Darrow, Clarence Seward
      and baseball, 19, 26
      birth, 14
      and bribery trial, 70–75
      and capital punishment,
      17, 41, 104–5
      childhood, 16–19
      death, 106
      and Debs trial, 47–49
      divorce, 54
      early years as lawyer, 22,
      25–27
      education, 18–20, 22
      final years, 102–6
      illness, 63
      and Leopold and Loeb
      trial, 79–87, 97, 99
      and McNamara trial, 67–
      70
      marriages, 23, 55
      move to Chicago, 29–35
      and politics, 27–28, 52–
      53
      and Prendergast trial, 40–
      41
      and religion, 13–15, 17,
      89, 93, 94, 102–3
      as schoolteacher, 20–21
      and Scopes trial, 11–15,
      89–97, 99
      and Western Federation
      of Miners trial, 59–63
Darrow, Edward Everett
   (brother), 17, 22, 29, 33
Darrow, Elizabeth (sister), 17

Darrow, Emily Eddy (mother),
   15, 20
Darrow, Herman (brother), 17
Darrow, Hubert (brother), 17
Darrow, Jennie (sister), 17
Darrow, Jessie Ohl (first wife),
   21, 23, 27, 29, 33, 34, 38,
   54
Darrow, Mary (sister), 17, 20,
   22
Darrow, Paul (son), 27, 29, 34,
   54, 99, 106
Darrow, Ruby Hamerstrom
   (second wife), 54–55, 67,
   71, 72, 74, 75, 77, 82,
   101, 103, 105
Darrow, William (brother), 17
Darwin, Charles, 12, 89, 90, 93
Dayton, Tennessee, 11–13,
   89, 91, 92, 94, 97
Debs, Eugene V., 44–45, 47–
   49, 66, 78–79
Democratic National Conven-
   tion of 1896, 52

Eddy, Burdett, 22
Evolution, theory of 12–13.
   See also Darrow,
   Clarence Seward: and
   Scopes trial

Farmdale, Ohio, 16
Farmington, 55
First Amendment, 91
Franklin, Bert, 68, 70, 72
Franks, Bobby, 79–80, 81, 85
Franks, Jacob, 79
Fredericks, John D., 69–72, 75
Freud, Sigmund, 83
Fundamentalists, 13, 89–90,
   94, 96

General Managers' Association, 45–46, 49
George, Henry, 33–34

Gompers, Samuel, 67, 71
Great Depression, 104
Great Northern Railroad, 45
Gregg, John H., 54
Gregory, S. S., 40, 47, 48

Hamerstrom, Ruby. *See* Darrow, Ruby Hamerstrom
Harlan, J. S., 40, 47
Harriman, Job, 69
Harrington, John, 68, 71, 72
Harrison, Carter, Sr., 31, 38–39
Haymarket Bombing, 31–32, 38
Haywood, "Big Bill," 56, 58, 60, 62
Holly, William H., 106
Holmes, John Haynes, 102
Honolulu, Hawaii, 103
Howard University, 100
Hughitt, Marvin, 38, 48

Insanity plea, 40

Kahahawaii, Joseph, 103–4
Kentucky, 90
Kinsman, Ohio, 15, 16, 17, 19, 20, 21, 23, 105
Kinsman Literary Society, 17–18
Kraus, Adolph, 39

Labor unions, 41–42. *See also* Pullman Company strike
Lincoln, Abraham, 26–27, 106
Leopold, Nathan, Jr., 79–87
Lockwood, George, 70–71
Loeb, Albert, 80, 82
Loeb, Richard ("Dickie"), 79–97
Los Angeles Times, 65–66

McCormick Reaper Works, 31
McKinley, William, 53
McManigal, Ortie, 66–70
McNamara, James, 66–70
McNamara, John J., 66–70
McParland, James, 57–58, 59
Malone, Dudley Field, 91
Massie, Thalia, 103
Massie, Thomas, 103–4
Masters, Edgar Lee, 67, 77
Mencken, Henry L., 106
Metcalf, Maynard M., 94
Michigan, University of, 22, 80
Monkey Trial. *See* Darrow, Clarence Seward: and Scopes trial
Morgan, Howard, 93, 94
Moyer, Charles, 58, 62
Murphy, Frank, 101, 102

National Association for the Advancement of Colored People (NAACP), 99, 100
National Industrial Recovery Act (NIRA), 104

Ohl, Jessie. *See* Darrow, Jessie Ohl
Olney, Richard, 46, 48
Orchard, Harry, 57–62
Otis, Harrison Gray, 65–66
Our Penal Machinery and Its Victims (Altgeld), 28–29

Pettibone, George, 58, 62
Prendergast, Eugene, 38–41
Pullman, George, 42–44, 48
Pullman City, 43–44, 49
Pullman Company strike, 42–49

Rappalyea, George, 90
Raulston, John, 13, 92–95, 97

Richards, Ralph C., 38
Richardson, Edmund, 60
Roberts, James, 23
Robinson, F. E., 90
Rogers, Earl, 72–74
Roosevelt, Franklin Delano, 104
Roosevelt, Theodore, 55

Scopes, John T., 13, 90, 91, 93–94, 97
Shelton, Harry, 94
Sherman, Laban S., 27
Simpkins, Jack, 58
Sissman, Peter, 77–78
Slavery, 16, 18
Southern Christian Fundamentalists, 90
Steffens, Lincoln, 71
Story of My Life, The, 27
Stuenenberg, Frank, 56–57, 61
Sweet, Henry, 100–102
Sweet, Ossian, 100–102
Sweet, Otis, 100–102

Trumbull, Lyman, 47

Underground Railroad, 18

Vernon, Ohio, 20

Walker, Edwin, 46, 48
Western Federation of Miners (WFM), 56, 58, 59, 63
White, Captain, 71
William J. Burns Detective Agency, 66, 68
Wilson, Francis, 67
Works Improvement Association, 101
World War I, 78

Youngstown, Ohio, 22

PICTURE CREDITS

John E. Driemen resides in Minneapolis and holds a master's degree in comparative literature from the University of Minnesota. He has had a long and varied career as a feature writer and as a film writer and director of educational and documentary motion pictures. He is the author of two other books for young readers: *Atomic Dawn: A Biography of Robert Oppenheimer* and *An Unbreakable Spirit: Winston Churchill*.

Vito Perrone is Director of Teacher Education and Chair of Teaching, Curriculum, and Learning Environments at Harvard University. He has previous experience as a public school teacher, a university professor of history, education, and peace studies (University of North Dakota), and as dean of the New School and the Center for Teaching and Learning (both at the University of North Dakota). Dr. Perrone has written extensively about such issues as educational equity, humanities curriculum, progressive education, and evaluation. His most recent books are: *A Letter to Teachers: Reflections on Schooling and the Art of Teaching*; *Enlarging Student Assessment in Schools*; *Working Papers: Reflections on Teachers, Schools, and Communities*; *Visions of Peace*; and *Johanna Knudsen Miller: A Pioneer Teacher*.